092645

973.92
Pau

DISCARD

SHELBYVILLE-SHELBY COUNTY
PUBLIC LIBRARY

The Thirty Years War

The Thirty Years War

The Politics of the Sixties Generation

A Memoir by
Thomas W. Pauken

JAMESON BOOKS, INC.
OTTAWA, ILLINOIS

SHELBYVILLE-SHELBY COUNTY
PUBLIC LIBRARY

Copyright © 1995 by Thomas W. Pauken
All rights reserved, including the right
to reproduce this book or portions thereof
in any form.

Published by Jameson Books, Inc.
722 Columbus Street, Ottawa, Illinois 61350.

Jameson Books are available at special discounts
for bulk purchases for sales promotions, premiums,
fund-raising, or educational use. Special editions,
condensed editions, or book excerpts can also
be created to specification. For details contact:
Special Sales Director, Jameson Books, Inc.,
P.O. Box 738, Ottawa, Illinois 61350
or call 815-434-7905.

Distributed to the book trade by
Login Brothers Consortium
1436 West Randolph Street
Chicago, Illinois 60607, 312-733-8228.

First Edition

1 3 5 6 4 2

ISBN: 0–915463–66–0

To my parents, whose support and sacrifices made possible the opportunities I have enjoyed.

To my wife Ida, who endured the long hours I spent writing this book, as we moved from place to place over the years, and whose love made time fly during our twenty-plus years together.

To my children, that they may understand why their Dad spent so much time fighting political battles whose significance often appeared hard for them to appreciate.

To Dr. George Carey of Georgetown, who helped me understand the genius of the American political system.

To Bill Bowen, friend and former boss, who led me to an appreciation of the entrepreneurial spirit which is the engine of our free enterprise system.

To Mike Joyce of the Harry and Lynde Bradley Foundation for essential support in the writing of this book.

And finally, to Pete Copp, friend and editor, whose help with this book encouraged me to persist even when it seemed it would never see the light of day.

Contents

Foreword

Newspaper accounts of the Texas State Republican Convention in June, 1994, described "the Christian Right's takeover of the party" which had become dominated by "intolerant religious zealots." The cataclysmic event so described was the election, defying the wishes of Texas party leaders, of Thomas W. Pauken as Republican state chairman.

Anybody who knows Tom Pauken, as I have for some 25 years, would have to chuckle to envision him as the Ayatollah of the Southwest, a Bible-belt Savonarola preaching theocracy and denying dissent. Pauken happens to be a practicing member of the Roman Catholic Church, an institution long viewed with fear and loathing by hard-shell Southern fundamentalists.

In truth, I did not even know Pauken was a Catholic until I read this book in page proofs. A political practitioner who has not shielded his opinions, he certainly has not worn his religion on his sleeve. He cares about many things, but theological conformity surely is not one of them. If evangelical Christians who have entered the Republican Party were obsessed by religious doctrine, they would not have selected him as the new party chairman.

Why Pauken's election caused so much heartburn is reflected in telephone conversations I placed to several old-line Texas Republicans after his election. The gist of their answers: "No, Tom certainly is no religious fanatic and not an extremist of any kind. But, well, he's sort of hard to get along with."

But the Tom Pauken I know is a most amiable gentleman, soft-spoken and non-confrontational. Nor is he pursuing an exotic agenda that is off somewhere on the far right fringe. He is a Ronald Reagan Republican, and that surely is smack in the mainstream of his party.

The *Thirty Years War* explains why so many Republicans find Pauken to be so prickly. Simply put, he believes in what he says, and performs accordingly. That is so rare in politics that he is something of an outcast. But what makes him an untouchable is his proclivity for saying the emperor has no clothes, if indeed the emperor happens to be naked. This book is filled with blunt declarations.

Nothing better demonstrates the Pauken style than how he related to Vietnam. As a young political activist and fervent Barry Goldwater supporter who worked his way up to the national chairmanship of the College Republicans, he vigorously backed U.S. participation in the war.

"I knew in my own mind that I would be nothing but a hypocrite if I ducked my own obligation to serve after being such an active supporter of the allied effort to defeat the Communists in Vietnam," he writes. So, rather than join his contemporaries—including not only his fellow Georgetown University student, Bill Clinton, but many professed war hawks as well—in playing the draft lottery game or joining the reserves in order to avoid combat, Pauken enlisted in the Army.

Once assigned to Vietnam, he found deplorable U.S. leadership of the war. But that did not drive him into disillusionment and cynicism—then or in the future. At a time when most conservatives would rather forget the war they supported, Pauken has remained deeply committed to the cause and to Vietnam veterans.

He returned from the war to work in the Nixon White House but once again was disappointed by what he saw. He found that President Nixon was a "corporate liberal" and concluded that "the Nixon White House made policy decisions based on who squawked the loudest or what the polls suggested ought to be done."

Comments such as these are the core of the Republican establishment's complaint about Pauken. But had there been more Paukens in the Nixon White House, Watergate and all that accompanied and followed it might well have been avoided. As a sober conservative, he was hostile to the mindset behind the proposed "Huston Plan," for what would have amounted to a domestic CIA. "It seemed," he writes, "as though a lot of people were running around the White House acting like 'super-spooks.'"

After Pauken left the Nixon White House and while Watergate was at full throttle, he was asked by fellow Texan George Bush— then Republican National Chairman—what he thought of the apostate John Dean's accusations against Nixon. "'I think that Dean may be telling the truth,' I responded. That wasn't what Bush wanted to hear, and our meeting ended shortly thereafter." Here was another mark against Pauken, branding him unreliable.

The next election of a Republican, Ronald Reagan, deeply stirred Pauken and the other Reaganauts. "It was an exciting moment; we conservatives were coming to Washington to dismantle the modern liberal state." But he soon found that many non-Reaganauts also were coming to Washington, and thanks to his reputation as a truth-teller, he was very nearly kept out of the Reagan Administration.

Only by the skin of his teeth did he win the nomination as head of ACTION, the federal agency in charge of volunteer activities, including the Peace Corps. He barely survived a confirmation fight, forced to defend himself because he had served as an Army intelligence officer in Vietnam. The price for confirmation was that the Peace Corps, under the direction of a liberal Bush protégé, was severed from ACTION.

I knew that Pauken was disliked by the secretariat at the White House run by another Texan, chief-of-staff James Baker. But I was not aware until I read this book just how much. Baker undercut him in dealing with left-wing activists, then killed an attempt by Ed Meese to put Pauken in charge of implementing the Grace Commission report to streamline government. Finally, Baker blocked his appointment as ambassador to the Caribbean Basin Initiative, effectively keeping Pauken out of the Reagan second-term administration.

Nobody has ever questioned Tom Pauken's ability, energy, or dedication. Considering the fact that he has been on the political scene for the 30 years of this book's title, he should be a major American political figure by now. But he has been unable to play the devious game that took his acquaintance at Georgetown, Bill Clinton, into the Oval Office and indeed is the accepted way of doing business in both parties.

Besides the battering he took in Washington, he lost four elections in Texas, but never lost his courage or his will. Rather than retreating into cynicism, he has always picked himself up and charged the ramparts again—often in a selfless cause. In 1993, after his last loss for Congress, a lesser man would have been discouraged, but he successfully led the way to defeat the "Robin Hood Amendment" to raise Texas school taxes and redistribute funds.

The reason his election as state party chairman caused apprehension among many old-line Republicans can be seen in what his vision was 30 years ago as a college student:

> Many of us never would have joined the party of Willkie, Dewey, Scranton, and Rockefeller, which was so closely identified with big business and Wall Street interests. Nor did we have much respect for upper class society types (or those trying to buy or wheedle their way into such circles) who were Republicans by birth or

Republicans for class reasons. We had left the majority party to become Republicans because of a commitment to conservative values.

Tom Pauken cherishes and nourishes the dangerous idea that the Republican Party should stand for something. He gives every indication that after fighting for 30 years, he is just getting his second wind.

ROBERT NOVAK
WASHINGTON, D.C.
AUGUST, 1994

Preface

Vietnam was the defining political issue of the sixties generation. It divided young Americans in a manner that we haven't seen in this country since the days of the Civil War. Now, with members of that generation moving into key positions of leadership in American society, one should not underestimate how much that war has shaped the thinking and beliefs of those of us who became political activists during the sixties.

We were a generation interested in, and involved in, politics. President Kennedy captured the allegiance of many young people with his vision of a New Frontier and his call to "ask not what your country can do for you, but what you can do for your country." Young conservatives helped pave the way for the nomination of Senator Barry Goldwater to be the Republican candidate for president in 1964. A group of youthful activists formed a political movement called the New Left and demanded the radical restructuring of American society. College students were in the forefront of the civil rights movement.

While all this political activity was going on, the war in Vietnam began to heat up. Campus conservatives and New Leftists already had clashed over a variety of political issues in their efforts to enlist the support of their fellow students. But it was the issue of Vietnam which turned these two formidable political movements into permanent adversaries.

There just wasn't any common ground with respect to our views about Vietnam. Those of us who called ourselves conservatives believed that we could, and should, have won that war in order to prevent a Communist takeover of South Vietnam. Our New Left opponents maintained that we were fighting on the wrong side in Vietnam and should have been supporting the Viet Cong guerrilla forces instead of the South Vietnamese government. Even today, it is difficult for leaders of both sides of that dispute to engage in a dialogue or come to a compromise on the subject of Vietnam.

Three decades later these two political movements—which can be classified as conservative populism and Left populism—continue their ongoing battle to shape the future of America. The leaders of the respective camps are a lot older, a little wiser, and more politically knowledgeable than they were back when they first squared off in the sixties. Yet the political differences within our generation are just as pronounced today on other issues as they were when we drew a line in the sand over Vietnam.

The student radicals won that political battle—their side prevailed in Vietnam. The young conservatives captured control of the Republican party—and finally were able to elect one of their own, Ronald Reagan, president in 1980. But these proved to be only temporary victories for the Left and the Right, respectively.

President Reagan was not able to reverse or stop the growth of big government. His successor, George Bush, never tried. Until Bill Clinton's election to the presidency in 1992, the New Left had been unable to put one of its own in the White House. Now Americans have a president who got his start in politics as an anti-Vietnam activist in the late sixties.

With Bill Clinton in the White House, that intragenerational fight for America's political future will heat up even more. This battle pits sixties conservatives and most Vietnam veterans against

New Left activists who remain committed to their objective of a radical transformation of American society.

It is truly a time for choosing sides.

I make no pretense of impartiality on this subject. I have been a participant in this political battle since I arrived at Georgetown University in 1961. My hope, obviously, is that the conservatives will win. But we may lose. Our opposition is formidable.

How and why we got to where we are is what this book is all about. There was something about the sixties that continues to shape America's political landscape. Where we go from here depends on the choices we make. I have made my choice. Hopefully this book will help you make yours.

1

For Duty, Honor, and Country

I arrived in South Vietnam on New Year's Day, 1969. The plane was packed with young soldiers, all of us trying our best to be nonchalant about what lay ahead of us. When we touched down at Bien Hoa airport, the heat and humidity were suffocating—quite a change from the winter weather back in the States.

At Long Binh we were transferred to our respective units. I was assigned to the 525 Military Intelligence (MI) group, an army unit in charge of intelligence collection and counterintelligence operations throughout South Vietnam.

This was my second trip to Vietnam, but the circumstances of this "visit" were quite different from my short stay in Saigon in the summer of 1966. Then, as the national chairman of the College Republicans and an outspoken supporter of our soldiers in Vietnam, I had been invited to go there and see firsthand what was going on. Our small group was given a series of briefings by American military and civilian advisers, including a session with General Edward Lansdale—the resident American expert with respect to Communist guerrilla insurgencies in Southeast Asia (and, allegedly, the person on whom the American hero is based in the best-selling novel *The Ugly American*). I even ran into a friend of mine who had been active in our College Republican organization and was now serving as a civilian adviser to the Agency for International Development. All of the government people we met on that visit were confident the Americans and our South Vietnamese allies would win the war against the Viet Cong and Ho Chi Minh's North Vietnamese Army.

I shared that optimism in 1966. My views had changed considerably, however, by the time I returned to Vietnam as a young army officer three years later.

Upon my arrival, I got in touch with Stu, a friend from army intelligence school at Fort Holabird in Baltimore who now was with a group called Strategic Research & Analysis in Saigon. Stu, I found, had had a rough go of it in the early months of his tour when he was running an agent network. A close friend and fellow case officer of his had walked into a Viet Cong ambush and was killed in what was supposed to be a friendly village. Stu arrived on the scene soon afterward and saw his dead companion. He never understood why the Vietnamese villagers hadn't given his friend a warning. He was so furious at what had happened that he was ready to burn the village down. Some of his fellow Americans had to restrain him. His feelings about the Vietnamese were never the same afterwards.

When he described how he felt, it was hard for me to believe that this was the same man who back at Holabird had been such a laid-back, easy going guy. Of all my classmates, Stu was the most antiwar. You wouldn't have expected that he would be tempted to strike back at the villagers in that way. But his buddy had been killed and he wanted revenge against the people who had done nothing to prevent it from happening.

It was easy to be an armchair quarterback in Washington, decrying the military excesses that took place during the war. How different it was to be in the midst of a war in which it was hard to tell your friends from your enemies and where sometimes those you believed to be friendly turned out to be your deadly foe. Stu told me he could arrange it so that I could be assigned to the Joint Intelligence Command in Saigon. As he put it, J2-SRA was good duty and the colonel who headed the unit was a good officer to work for.

Having come all this way to Vietnam, however, I figured that I might as well get out into the field and see a side of the war that I wouldn't learn about if I stayed in Saigon my entire tour. So, I opted to serve as a "case operator" out in the field. I soon received orders for the Fourth Battalion headquartered in Can Tho, the center of the Delta.

The initial briefing I received from the Fourth Battalion executive officers was disappointing, and gave me the uneasy feeling that these men weren't professionals. Instead, they appeared to be officers more in the military bureaucratic mold, intent on impressing their superiors in Saigon by playing what some of us called "the numbers game." The officer in charge of intelligence operations, whom one of the young enlisted men had dubbed "Captain America," proudly emphasized that the quantity of agent reports filed by the Fourth Battalion was on the rise. That was his way of measuring the success of the unit's efforts. "Oh, no," I thought, "I've gotten stuck in Vietnam working for careerist types more concerned about personal advancement in rank than about winning the war."

I already had shed myself of any illusions that the military had all the answers when it came to prosecuting the war, or that its management of the war was what it was represented to be. Back home, the army's Defense Language Institute in El Paso, Texas, where I received my training in Vietnamese, provided nowhere near the caliber of language instruction that students received at Monterey, California, where the army's main instruction in languages took place. This was just one example of an overextended military having trouble coping with the need to train large numbers of young soldiers to satisfy our Vietnam manpower requirements. The military officials running the Vietnamese school in El Paso could hardly keep up with the demand for language-trained servicemen. The quality of instruction suffered; by and large, we were not achieving the level of proficiency expected under such an intense program.

When I was at El Paso, the word apparently had gotten back to the headquarters group that the army's language school there was not up to par. One day it was announced that some prominent officials from Washington would be inspecting the school within a few weeks. The word was quietly passed that when the visitors from Washington came into the classroom, the students should be speaking Vietnamese with their instructor or fellow students. It didn't matter what was said so long as the words sounded Vietnamese because the Washington officials did not understand the language anyway.

This occurred around the time that Republican presidential candidate George Romney made national headlines on his return from a trip to Vietnam. The Michigan governor claimed that American military advisers there had attempted to "brainwash" him. The statement proved so damaging to Romney that his presidential campaign went into a tailspin from which it never recovered. Had he simply stated that the military had tried to give him a snow job over there, the American public (particularly those with prior military service) would have gotten Romney's point—that the situation in Vietnam was not as much under control as the military wanted him to believe.

For all practical purposes, those of us at the language school were being asked to do the same thing that Romney was accusing military officials in Vietnam of doing—pulling the wool over the eyes of some Washington officials by making the training program appear to be better than it actually was. If some military careerists would go to such lengths to cover up a deficiency in Vietnamese language training at a remote post in El Paso, Texas, then it was hardly surprising to discover that officials were doing something similar in Vietnam where the stakes were much higher.

This relatively minor instance in which senior officers tried to mislead their own superiors had an effect upon my attitude toward career military officers. Up until then, I had persuaded myself that most career officers took seriously the principles of "duty, honor, and country," and had as their primary goal the defeat of the Communists in South Vietnam. After all, isn't that why I had volunteered for service in Vietnam, when I could have enlisted in the guard or reserves and almost certainly escaped going over-seas? Now, I was exposed to a different breed of military officers who viewed what they were doing as little more than a job they were determined to protect at all costs. It became much more difficult for me to accept as the "gospel truth" assessments of the situation in Vietnam mouthed by senior military officials.

Now here I was in the Fourth Battalion with "Captain America." In his briefings of new officers and visitors from Saigon, Captain America was particularly proud of an agent from Long Xuyen, a province in the southwest portion of the Delta not far from the Cambodian border. According to the captain, this particular Vietnamese agent was a "Catholic anti-Communist" who had an extensive network of agents working for him in Cambodia. He was supplying us with a number of reports from his extensive network of subagents on a steady basis. From the captain's per-spective, this man was the Fourth Battalion of the 525 MI group's most "productive" agent.

I was assigned to handle Our Man from Long Xuyen and soon had my first meeting with this "staunch foe of Communism." I was excited about finally getting to do the work I had been trained for and hopefully making a difference in the war.

In spite of having studied Vietnamese, I was not fluent in the language and was assigned a Vietnamese interpreter named Son, whose Americanized name was Rio. We would be together for much of the year, which was my good fortune since Rio was an experienced and dedicated operative. I came to rely heavily on his instincts and judgment about intelligence matters. He had previously worked with the American Green Berets. Since fam-ily members of his had been killed by the Viet Cong, Rio had no illusions about the "progressive" nature of a potential Communist regime in the South.

We met with Our Man from Long Xuyen at a safe house, and I spent a lot of time reviewing his various agent networks in Cambodia and the information these operatives were providing us. The more questions I asked, the more concerned I became with the vagueness and unresponsiveness of his answers. Suddenly, I had a bad feeling that I might have an intelligence fabricator on my hands. I talked with my interpreter after the meeting, and he had a similar reaction. Something was not quite right about our "Catholic anti-Communist."

As I reviewed the information being provided by this agent it soon became clear that, while he was sending in a voluminous number of reports from his network in Cambodia, most of it was dated, low-level information that would be virtually impossible to react to or to confirm. My suspicions aroused, I persuaded my superiors to let me take a trip to Saigon to check out this man with other intelligence agencies.

Our Man from Long Xuyen was right in asserting that he had been involved in intelligence work for a long time. As it turned out, he had been terminated by the French in the fifties and, later, by the CIA for fabricating information. Now, he was making his living by conning the army intelligence boys into paying him a bunch of money for himself and a group of nonexistent agents.

Later, whenever my interpreter and I would drive through Long Xuyen in our jeep, we would pass by the chicken farm of our former agent, funded, I am sure, by American intelligence dollars. I had gotten a rude welcome to the subterranean world of the Vietnamese war effort, where reality was often far different from surface appearances.

By now, I wasn't sure what to believe. I just knew that I had the good part of a year left to serve "in country" and was determined to make the best of what by then was becoming a war filled with ambiguities: deception, mismanagement, runaway emotions, selfish goals, a lack of principle. I volunteered for active duty in this war. Had I made the right decision? After all, this was a place from which many a young soldier never returned.

Looking back, my road to Vietnam had been a long one. It began during my freshman year at Georgetown University when I joined the effort to build a conservative movement on campus. We were Goldwater Republicans. Our conservative philosophy was a deeply rooted conviction about what was right and what wasn't. We were activists promoting a return to policies that we were convinced had made America great.

By the time I was elected national chairman of the College Republicans, the Vietnam War had become a hot issue. I found myself in debates and teach-ins all over the country, battling the

New Left wherever I went. My message was clear: nothing less than a Communist defeat was morally acceptable. As the mood around the campuses, in the press, and indeed, across the country, soured, I had to face the decision that would forever change my life. How could I debate the merits of our involvement in Vietnam, where young men my age were fighting and dying, without going there? How could I accept a student deferment that kept me out of a conflict I supported?

My convictions and conscience left me no choice.

2

Vietnam: 1969

There's an old saying about "shooting the messenger who brings the bad news." Needless to say, the reaction at headquarters to my news that their "top agent" had turned out to be a phony wasn't warmly received by Captain America. This operative had been cited repeatedly in briefings as one of the "prize" examples of the intelligence-gathering successes of the Fourth Battalion. I began to suspect that I might have to pay a price for my indelicate discovery of this con man by being stuck with menial work at headquarters in Can Tho for the duration of my tour of duty.

Neither the captain nor the executive officer, whom some of us called Major Major (a name we borrowed from a character in Joseph Heller's book *Catch 22*), were the type of military officers who inspired a young lieutenant like me, who wanted to do his job and go home. So, I knew that I had to get out of the headquarters office soon before saying or doing something that would get me in more trouble with my superiors.

Fortunately, I was able to talk my way into an assignment to run a collection operation out of Chau Doc, a province which bordered on Cambodia and (conveniently) was a good distance from Can Tho. There, at the end of the line of the intelligence-gathering network of 525 MI, is when and where I began to get a feel for what was really going on in Vietnam.

I had received first-rate training in intelligence collection at army intelligence school at Fort Holabird and was well prepared for this assignment. The instructors at Holabird were professionals who knew their business, in dramatic contrast to my previous instructors in basic training at Fort Bragg, North Carolina, and again later at the Defense Language Institute. At Holabird I studied under some of the most experienced and successful intelligence operatives in the military.

Practically speaking, I was my own boss in Chau Doc, and since my "cover" was that of a civilian Defense Department employee, my assignment gave me freedom to travel the Delta and assess the overall status of the war effort from a fairly unique vantage point. Working directly with Vietnamese and ethnic Cambodians for much of my tour of duty, I could observe the Byzantine political and religious undercurrents in Vietnamese society.

My initial mission was to set up a new intelligence-gathering network since our only unilateral operation in this part of the Delta was now defunct. Intelligence operations were classified as unilateral or bilateral depending on whether we ran the networks solely as an American enterprise (unilateral) or collaborated with our South Vietnamese allies in running agents (bilateral). Our man from Long Xuyen had been a unilateral operation, and we needed to replace him with a new principal agent who we hoped would have access to Communist military targets in Cambodia.

As a province intelligence officer, I also took on responsibilities for studying the political side of the war since my cover was that of a Department of Defense analyst for a research organization known as the Field Test Unit. Ironically, my cover as an analyst ultimately assumed a larger than anticipated role in my intelligence work in the Delta. To make my cover believable and to learn more about the intricacies of Vietnamese politics, I quickly got to know a number of religious and political leaders in the region.

I worked closely with members of one of the leading Buddhist sects in South Vietnam, the Hoa Hao Buddhists, whose headquarters were in the province of Long Xuyen, a short distance from Chau Doc. As a result, I gained a better appreciation for the political role assumed by many religious groups in South Vietnam. Since political parties had been frowned upon in the past when Vietnam was under foreign dominance, a variety of religious groups had emerged which assumed many of the functions of political organizations. In the case of the Hoa Hao, this religious group had an extensive organizational structure, its own private army, and its own taxing system.

It became readily apparent to me after dealing with various Hoa Hao leaders, that many of them had agendas other than the advancement of their religion. One senior Hoa Hao leader, whom I got to know quite well, was an opium smuggler in addition to his official religious duties. He was quite an operator. This is not to suggest that there weren't many dedicated adherents to the Hoa Hao faith among those Vietnamese who had embraced that belief system. Nonetheless, some of their leaders had political and economic agendas which influenced their actions more than their professed belief in Hoa Hao Buddhism.

We tried to recruit one such Hoa Hao leader, who was a real "wheeler dealer," as an agent. In addition to serving as a high-ranking lay leader in one of the two major factions within the Hoa Hao religion, our prospective agent was involved in a variety of business enterprises. Factionalism was rampant in virtually every institution within South Vietnamese society, and the Hoa Hao sect was no exception to this general phenomenon.

Our new prospective agent and I got along well. After we became better acquainted, I approached him about working for American intelligence and providing information on Communist political and military targets in the Delta and in Cambodia. He made it clear to me that he didn't want to work for the South Vietnamese government since the relationship between the Hoa Hao leaders and Vietnamese officialdom was strained. He assumed that I worked for the American CIA, and I did nothing to dissuade him from that notion since he was very impressed with the professionalism and money the CIA had available to pay its agents.

After getting approval from headquarters to recruit my Hoa Hao contact, I went to pick him up in Long Xuyen in our Fourth Battalion helicopter. I was taking him to Saigon to meet a "senior" official of our organization and finalize our working relationship. He was suitably impressed that the Americans were going to such lengths to "recruit" him. All was going smoothly until our helicopter developed engine trouble, and our pilot was forced to make a crash landing in a Viet Cong-infested area in the Delta. We scrambled out of the chopper once it had banged to the ground, and were very relieved when other American helicopters arrived on the scene within minutes to rescue us and take us back to the Can Tho air base.

There was only one problem. With the only helicopter available to the Fourth Battalion now out of service, I had no way to get our new recruit to Saigon. I tried everything possible to arrange for another helicopter, or for any available air transportation at the base, to take our man from Can Tho to Saigon. For security reasons, while I could hop a plane ride to Saigon, only Vietnamese with security clearances were permitted on military planes and choppers flying in and out of this airfield. I had to tell our prospective agent that he had to catch a bus to Saigon.

By the time we held our meeting in a hotel room in Saigon, I could tell that my Hoa Hao contact had changed his attitude about working with us. If these Americans couldn't even produce another helicopter after the first one went down or get him on an Air America plane (which was known by nearly everyone to be a CIA-run airline), then surely he wasn't dealing with very important American intelligence officials. Moreover, when the senior American operative I had arranged to meet him in Saigon (who was in reality a warrant officer) turned out not to be a mental match for him, that was all my Vietnamese contact needed to conclude that working with this group of Americans wouldn't be worth his while.

Still, my time in Chau Doc turned out to be productive even though we weren't able to recruit our "big fish." I lived in a civilian compound not too far from the American military headquarters. In this region, Americans generally were advisers to the South Vietnamese military, and most of the small contingent of Americans in Chau Doc were attached to various Vietnamese units. By and large, the American advisers were a good, solid group of people who were doing their best to "win the war." Like myself, they worked on an ongoing basis with Vietnamese and developed good relationships with people involved in a common cause.

Our compound was located near a South Vietnamese artillery battery, and you had to get used to the "outgoing" and "incoming" most evenings. What was frustrating to us was that the enemy was shelling us from their sanctuaries in Cambodia, and we weren't allowed to retaliate. Fortunately, our military developed a flexible approach of returning fire when shelled from across the border. The previous resident of the room I was given had been evacuated when he was injured as a result of an enemy shelling. Thankfully, the Communist artillery guns had not locked into that particular site again, so there weren't any further direct hits while I was there.

Frustrated by official reports on the state of the war and most of the media coverage coming out of Vietnam, I set down my own views on the war in a letter to an old Asian hand named DeWitt "Pete" Copp who had befriended me when I was national chairman of the College Republicans. Pete had been the editor of the American Security Council *Washington Report* and had published an article of mine on the New Left in 1966. We had stayed in touch over the years, and he had asked me for my observations on what was going on in Vietnam. In summary, I wrote that while I hoped we would win the war, I was afraid that we were going to lose if we kept on our current course.

Pete wrote back and asked if I would mind if he shared my thoughts with a friend of his, Grant Salisbury, who was an editor at *U.S. News & World Report*. I had no objection since all I had written down were my observations concerning the political side of the war. I figured that he might want to take a line or two out of what I had written to insert in a longer piece on the war.

At about this time, I was in poor health. My weight was down to about 120 pounds, and I was constantly dehydrated. Exhausted, I knew that something was wrong. I finally went to the hospital at Cam Ranh Bay where a doctor diagnosed my condition as amoebic dysentery. My assignment necessitated eating out quite often in the Delta where health conditions at the various restaurants were less than ideal, and I had picked up a bug at one of these spots.

A week later, I was released from the hospital and sent back to the headquarters unit in Can Tho in a still weakened but improved condition. With only a little more than four months remaining until DEROS, I was afraid that I was going to be a headquarters staff officer for the remainder of my tour.

The people at Strategic Research & Analysis (SRA) wanted me to join their unit, but I was having a difficult time getting my superiors in Can Tho to approve my transfer. I was not the most popular first lieutenant at Fourth Battalion. Fortunately, the powers that be decided they would rather have me out of their hair, and I was permitted to leave for the SRA office at the Joint Intelligence Command at MACV headquarters in Saigon.

There, I had the good fortune to serve under an outstanding officer, Col. Chieu Man Lee (whom his men called Chairman Lee). Colonel Lee had been awarded the Silver Star in the Korean War, and he knew how to get the most out of the young officers and enlisted men who were working for him. Morale in the office was high; during the time I spent there, I worked with some of the smartest and most capable people with whom I have ever been associated.

My own productivity went way up. The time I had spent in the Delta served me well as it gave me insights into certain issues that I wouldn't have had if I had spent my entire tour in Saigon. I didn't look at everything from just the Saigon perspective, a trap which some analysts and journalists fell into. I worked on issues ranging from the targeting of religious groups in South Vietnam by the Viet Cong, to North Vietnamese revolutionary strategy as set forth by Truong Chinh, the leading Communist strategist in North Vietnam. It was a very rewarding job, marred only by one incident which threatened to create some problems for me.

The letter I had sent my friend Pete Copp from Chau Doc appeared in a highly publicized article in *U.S. News & World Report* entitled "State of the War: An Intelligence Report." Although no sensitive material had been included, the publicity on the story emphasized the inside tenor of the information. Besides, the conclusion of the piece was that, unless we changed our policy in Vietnam, we were not likely to win the war.

As soon as I saw the article, I went to my commanding officer, Colonel Lee, and told him that I was the culprit. I explained the circumstances of my original letter to Pete Copp and said that I hadn't anticipated that my observations would show up in this form. He couldn't have been more gracious about what had happened and said that, as far as he was concerned, it was a dead issue.

Some senior officers at MACV headquarters were intent on discovering the identity of the author of the article. A lieutenant colonel got close to the truth when he said to one of our officers at Strategic Research & Analysis that the article looked like something one of our people would write. Then, he focused on a report that I had written for SRA and asked our executive officer, "Who authored that particular study?" The officer's response was that the study was a group effort like most of our studies. Thus, I was saved from a possibly acrimonious confrontation with one career officer who didn't like what I had written. As I had only a short while left in Vietnam before going home, I was very grateful to Colonel Lee and his executive officer for taking care of one of their men when it would have been more convenient for them to hang me out to dry.

3

Life Seemed So Much Simpler Then

There was a popular television commercial for Chevrolet a number of years back that portrayed the "good old USA" as an idyllic land. Part of the jingle that accompanied the pictures went something like this: "baseball, hot dogs, apple pie, and Chevrolet." After spending nearly a year in Vietnam, an idealized vision of America similar to that of the Chevy commercial, was something to cling to as the clock wound down on your tour.

It is hard to describe my feelings as I boarded the plane at Saigon's Tan Sanh Nhut airport bound for America. Arriving at the military process center at Oakland, California, in late December, 1969, all I wanted to know was where to sign to get out of the Army. From my perspective, I had done my part and was eager to resume life as a civilian. Most of the other young, returning veterans felt the same way.

A day later, I was "free." A military bus took me to the San Francisco airport where I would catch a flight home to Dallas. Waiting for my plane to leave, I couldn't believe my eyes as I watched the people trooping in and out of the terminal. Either America wasn't the same anymore, or I was different.

The "flower children" seemed to be out in force with their long hair and "hippie-style" dress. Many of these young people were wearing peace symbols of one kind or another, signaling their opposition to the war. The times were, indeed, changing.

As a kid growing up in America during the relatively tranquil fifties, I had no inkling of how different the sixties would turn out to be when I went off to college in 1961. Who would have been so bold as to predict that the quiet stability of the Eisenhower years (whose youthful generation had been characterized as the "silent generation") would give way to a wave of political activism on college campuses in the sixties. "Political activism" and "Vietnam" were far from my mind during my grade school and high school years in Dallas. Baseball was my principal interest, from following my favorite team, the New York Yankees, to playing shortstop on a boys' baseball team while dreaming of one day playing that same position in the major leagues and following in the footsteps of my favorite Yankee player, Phil Rizzuto.

We were the "baby boomers" generation, children of adults whose parents were shaped by the Great Depression, the Franklin Roosevelt era, and World War II. The fifties were the Eisenhower years and "we liked Ike" just as our parents did. The former commander of Allied forces during World War II, President Eisenhower was a grandfatherly figure who made Americans feel safe and secure during his years in the White House (1953 to 1961).

The American family as an institution was still intact then, and most of us who attended Christ the King grade school were products of a family where the father worked while the mother stayed at home with the kids. The middle-class dream was to own your own home, and I still remember our family's excitement when my dad bought a lot and built our house in what was then far north Dallas.

Politically in the fifties, most people seemed to share a common set of values. Of course, within that framework, there were substantial differences between liberals and conservatives on individual issues. But when it came down to basic attitudes concerning patriotism, religion, military service, or our system of government, there was a widespread consensus among Americans. The linchpin of that value system was our belief in God. As Supreme Court Justice William O. Douglas noted in an opinion in a case before the high Court: "We are a religious people whose institutions presuppose the existence of a Supreme Being." The Judeo-Christian ethic was the standard by which our conduct was to be measured.

As for political parties, we really had three strong factions in the fifties—conservative Democrats (generally from the South), liberal Democrats, and Republicans. In my home state of Texas, for all practical purposes, we had only two parties under the umbrella of the Texas Democratic party: conservative Democrats and liberal Democrats. The Republican party at the time was an insignificant force, still paying the political price for what the carpetbaggers in the name of Republicanism had done to the South during Reconstruction.

Conservative Democrats in Texas were led in the fifties by the last great Democratic governor of our state, Allen Shivers, who headed Dwight Eisenhower's campaign for the presidency in Texas in 1952 and 1956. The leader of the liberal Democrats in Texas was Ralph Yarborough who won election to the United States Senate in 1958.

The fifties were the early days of television, and candidates for office would go on the air for thirty minutes at a time to try to get their message out to the voters. It was fascinating to watch these politicians use television to talk directly to the people, unlike today when all we are likely to get are thirty-second sound bites. That was my first real exposure to politicians, and after watching them speak, I felt that at least I had a cursory understanding of what they stood for and what they were like as human beings. Even if your perception of the candidate was only partially accurate, that opportunity to observe candidates in an unfiltered setting allowed you to make a far more educated choice when it came to voting than one can today when high-priced media consultants package candidates as they would package a grocery product in slick thirty-second spots.

Just as politics were simpler then, so too was religion. I grew up in a traditional Catholic environment with nuns teaching in grade school and old-style priests instructing us at Jesuit High School. In elementary school, we were taught the basic tenets of the Roman Catholic faith as spelled out in the Baltimore Catechism. It was a Ten Commandments approach to religion which set forth clear rules we as Christians were supposed to follow. While we learned soon enough that we might occasionally fail to live up to these standards, our failures (or sins, if you will) didn't change our fundamental beliefs. The Jesuits built on these fundamentals by teaching us the intellectual underpinnings of our faith through the study of such great theologians as Thomas Aquinas, whose proofs of the existence of God were a major focus of my senior theology course under Father Cullen, S.J.

The foundation I received from family and schools made the Christian faith seem perfectly logical and coherent to me by the time I headed off to Georgetown University. I was already gaining a reputation for what a Soviet Intourist guide later called my "excessive individualistic" tendencies, but when it came to matters of religion, my high school years made me comfortable both intellectually and emotionally with Catholicism.

My Jesuit High School education also had an influence on me in other areas. As a freshman, I had wanted to continue playing baseball. But my freshman teacher, Fr. Jacques Weber, S.J., recruited me for the debate team and informed me that I couldn't debate and also be on the baseball team. I was in a real quandary. After all, I was being asked to give up my dream...every kid's dream of playing in the big leagues someday. But Father Weber's "Jesuitical logic" was convincing when he pointed out to me that a kid who had a .250 batting average in the boys baseball league didn't stand much of a chance to make the big leagues. Reality quickly set in, and that was the end of my dream of playing for the Yankees.

I immediately threw myself into the debate team with the fervor I previously had reserved for sports. Participating in debate under a great coach like Father Weber was a tremendous intellectual discipline for me. It forced me to study both sides of the issues we debated since we alternated between the affirmative and negative sides at each tournament. I learned how to think and express myself in a logical fashion, and to analyze public policy issues from differing perspectives. This constant exposure to arguments on both sides of major issues encouraged my already developing interest in politics, and also led me ultimately to the realization that my political philosophy was basically conservative, although I wasn't quite sure what "being conservative" meant yet.

This didn't mean that I was comfortable with the status quo since I was already skeptical of the influence of certain major institutions in our society—big government, big business, and big labor. Nor was I wildly enthusiastic about the presidential candidacy of Richard Nixon, who was ostensibly the more conservative candidate for president in his 1960 race against John F. Kennedy. While I didn't agree with Kennedy's politics, to me he was a more likable human being. Moreover, as a Catholic, I resented the apparent use of the religious issue against Kennedy.

I still remember the moment when watching that first televised debate between Kennedy and Nixon, I sensed for the first time that Kennedy would win the election. The questioner asked both candidates what they thought of former President Harry Truman's recent comment that "Republicans were SOBs." Kennedy handled the reporter's stupid question in a deft manner by simply shrugging it off with a comment along the lines that, well, that's just the way Harry Truman is and he is not likely to change at this stage in his life. In effect Kennedy was saying that everyone knows that this is a typical comment one might expect from old "give 'em hell Harry."

By contrast, Richard Nixon gave a sanctimonious response to the question, saying that Mr. Truman's language was offensive to the "mothers of America." Nixon's answer had a false ring to it, and I suspect that many other viewers had a reaction similar to my own. Also, in the first debate, Nixon struck me as a "me too" Republican, agreeing with Kennedy's basic premise of a more "activist" federal government, but arguing that we should go slower than Kennedy proposed and that he could manage the federal government better than Kennedy. It was not a particularly inspiring performance so, while I supported Nixon as the more conservative of the two candidates, it was with little personal enthusiasm. Issues, however, were pushing me in the direction of the Republican party, particularly because of my strong opposition to Communism around the world and my belief that Republicans were stronger foes of the Soviet empire.

4

A Young Conservative Goes to Washington

I arrived at Georgetown University in Washington, D.C., as a seventeen-year-old freshman during the first year of the Kennedy administration.

Founded in 1789 by Jesuits, Georgetown is the oldest Catholic university in the United States. Before I attended school there, it had earned a well-deserved reputation for educational excellence. Georgetown had managed to preserve its unique identity as a religious-based university long after its Ivy League counterparts like Harvard and Yale had shed their last remaining connection with the religious denominations responsible for their founding.

Six hundred of us entered the then all-male College of Arts and Sciences in 1961, with most of us managing to graduate four years later. Georgetown benefited from being situated in our nation's capital, but attending school there was still a bit like being part of a separate, close-knit community within Washington. We got to know most of our classmates, and our professors were easily accessible to us. It was a true "academic community" where ideas mattered.

Georgetown definitely was not a member in good standing of the Liberal Establishment "club" when I arrived on campus in the fall of 1961. The university still had an unapologetic religious character to it. The first book assigned to us as incoming freshmen was John Henry Newman's classic, *The Idea of a University*, which made the case that an institution entrusted with the education of college students should be guided by a search for truth. The emphasis in theology and philosophy was on the thought of men like Aristotle, Augustine, Thomas Aquinas, Etienne Gilson, and G. K. Chesterton.

My American government and political theory professor was George Carey, one of the finest political scientists in the United States. Through Dr. Carey and his mentor, the late Willmoore Kendall, I gained a deep appreciation for the American political tradition. We read and reread James Madison, Alexander Hamilton, and John Jay, authors of *The Federalist*, a document that defines this political system of ours as well as any written source.

These men knew that people aren't angels. Thus, the authors of the Constitution sought to establish a political system which would limit and diffuse the power of government. Students of Dr. Carey gained an appreciation for the genius of the American Constitution and the delicate system of checks and balances and separation of powers which held it together.

We also studied *We Hold These Truths*, a book on the American political experience by the Jesuit priest John Courtney Murray. Father Murray argued that the political principles of our Founding Fathers are just as pertinent today as they were at the time of our founding. Murray noted:

> For the pragmatist there are, properly speaking, no truths; there are only results. But the American Proposition rests on the more traditional conviction that there are truths; that they can be known; that they must be held; for, if they are not held, assented to, consented to, worked into the texture of institutions, there can be no hope of founding a true City, in which

men may dwell in dignity, peace, unity, justice, well-being, freedom.

It was an exciting time to be an undergraduate at Georgetown. In addition to studying under professors like George Carey who challenged them intellectually, the students who made up the Class of 1965 were a solid and down-to-earth group, most of whom never took themselves too seriously. There was a special sense of community that permeated life at Georgetown in those days.

My years at Georgetown were the beginning of what would turn out to be a lifetime involvement in politics. New Frontier liberalism was in vogue then, both at Georgetown and among the opinion leaders in our nation's capital. There was an infectious air of optimism in the city that the Kennedy administration would pull America out of the lethargy into which it supposedly had lapsed during the Eisenhower years. Already, some pundits were heralding the Kennedy years as the new age of Camelot. The "best and the brightest" had arrived in Washington to run the government.

The New Frontiersmen who descended on the city in 1961 had an absolute confidence in their ability to accomplish whatever they set out to do. They firmly believed in the precepts of liberalism, most particularly in "the idea of progress—the belief that man, by the aid of science, can achieve a perfection of living limited only by the imaginative powers of the mind," as Whittaker Chambers defined it. This illusion that the New Frontiersmen could reshape human nature both at home and abroad in their quest to build a better world was doomed to failure, though at the time it seemed as if there were nothing but clear sailing ahead.

(I distinguish here the traditional brand of liberalism emanating from Woodrow Wilson through Franklin Delano Roosevelt, Harry Truman, John F. Kennedy, and Lyndon Johnson [and known as the New Deal, the Fair Deal, the New Frontier, and the Great Society] from the sixties-style, secular leftism which revolted against the dominant cultural values of American society. Hereinafter, I will refer to this force as the New Left, a title that movement gave itself in the sixties.)

The Jesuits on campus got caught up in the excitement of this young, Catholic president ready to take Washington by storm. An

SHELBYVILLE-SHELBY COUNTY
PUBLIC LIBRARY

article in our campus newspaper reported that all twenty of the Jesuits in residence at Georgetown had supported John Kennedy in the 1960 election.

Instead of joining what then appeared the winning side of American politics, I became a foot soldier in a small but steadily growing conservative army which was winning converts among college students and young people across the country.

The political leader of the movement was a Republican senator from Arizona, Barry Goldwater. His stirring address at the 1960 Republican National Convention had turned him into a national political figure overnight and effectively made him the leader of the conservative forces.

Goldwater's message appealed to young people like me. He spoke up for the individual in a society increasingly dominated by large, impersonal institutions. He stirred the idealistic instincts of young people who sensed that America somehow was coming unraveled. Goldwater articulated that feeling so many of us had that America was heading in the wrong direction, and that the time had come to return to our traditional American roots.

Idealism, rugged individualism, moral convictions, a return to traditional American values—all were chords Goldwater tapped as he emerged as the principal political spokesman for the new wave of conservatism. Within the Republican party, Goldwater became the point man for a major political revolt against the Eastern political and financial Establishment which had long dominated the party structure. Goldwater did what so few politicians are willing to do—he talked about issues in terms of black and white, rather than the grays people were accustomed to hearing. It was refreshing to hear such talk from a man in politics.

No one could have complemented Goldwater more effectively than William F. Buckley, Jr., the controversial young editor of the conservative magazine *National Review*. Buckley burst the liberal bubble.

Many liberals have a tendency to view themselves and their philosophy as intellectually superior to those of us who call ourselves conservatives. That sort of bias against conservatives as "simplistic reactionaries" was far worse back in the early sixties (although it still remains a significant problem for conservatives today) when there were so few intellectuals on the American scene making the case for the conservative philosophy. Particularly then, liberal professors on the campuses tended to reject conservative arguments out of hand as not being worthy of serious discussion. A combination of intellectual arrogance, closemindedness, and prejudice against the conservative philosophy led sixties-style liberals to dismiss this new political movement on the right as little more than a fad which would quickly fade away.

An unapologetic defender of conservatism and caustic critic of the Liberal Establishment, Bill Buckley was the "bad boy" of the conservative movement. As a young graduate of Yale University, in 1951 Buckley created a furor at his alma mater with his book *God and Man at Yale,* a scathing attack on the irreligious and antireligious values being taught in the classrooms at Yale. He followed that up shortly with a defense of Senator Joe McCarthy in a book he co-authored with his brother-in-law Brent Bozell, *McCarthy and His Enemies.*

Buckley loved to use the line in his speeches before campus audiences about how he would prefer to be governed by the first two thousand names in the Boston telephone directory than the two thousand members of the faculty at Harvard University. That remark got quite a laugh from his non-Ivy League campus audiences. The Liberals, so accustomed to poking fun at a sitting target (the stodgy big business Establishment) suddenly found themselves on the receiving end of barbs delivered by an anti-Establishment conservative intellectual who had the audacity to accuse the intellectual majority of being part of an establishment of its own. And he even gave it a name—"the Eastern Liberal Establishment." It was enough to give liberals fits.

A year before I arrived at Georgetown, the Jesuits had refused to allow Buckley to speak on campus because his conservative views were considered "too extreme."

Buckley and Goldwater made quite a team for the conservatives. Barry Goldwater was the political leader and Bill Buckley was the intellectual leader of this embryonic movement. In addition to their public appearances on campuses throughout the country, they were the authors of two books which were widely read by young conservatives—the best seller *The Conscience of a Conservative* by Goldwater (which was ghosted for him by Brent Bozell) and Buckley's *Up from Liberalism.*

Goldwater and Buckley began playing to packed houses on college campuses wherever they spoke. At Georgetown, eight hundred students crowded into Gaston Hall to listen to Goldwater. Students responded enthusiastically to Goldwater's conservative message. Buckley likewise was warmly received by college audiences, although faculty members and university administrators more often than not were openly hostile to his conservative message.

Bill Buckley finally got to speak at Georgetown during my undergraduate years in spite of the continued efforts on the part of some Jesuits to block his visit. One left-wing Jesuit, Fr. Richard McSorley, was so adamantly opposed to Buckley's appearance at Georgetown that he went all over campus tearing down posters announcing the time and place of the Buckley speech. But it was all to no avail as students filled Gaston Hall to the rafters to hear Buckley's address.

His remarks that evening were enthusiastically received by the students even though (or perhaps because) one of the Georgetown professors spent a lot of time during the question and answer period trying to show Buckley up as a political extremist. (These days, the expression would be that Buckley's views were "politically incorrect.") The professor in question lost that debate, insofar as the audience was concerned. You could sense the excitement in the air. A conservative phenomenon was beginning to take hold among the young, and many of us at Georgetown got caught up in the fervor and idealism of the moment, which most experts at the time considered to be simply another lost cause.

A group of us underclassmen took it upon ourselves to reorganize a nearly defunct Young Republican Club on campus. We had very few members at the beginning and practically no money to spend on organizational efforts. There weren't any senior Republicans looking over our shoulders to show us how to get organized or giving us money to aid our efforts. We were on our own and learned by a process of trial and error. We didn't know that our goal of building a large conservative organization on the campus of a Catholic university in our nation's capital during the administration of the first Catholic president must have seemed to others a quixotic undertaking.

T. A. Quinn was part of that small corps of conservatives. A junior from the wine country of northern California, T. A. wrote a conservative political column for the *Hoya,* the campus newspaper. T. A. was a gifted writer who also was well-organized; that was a big plus since organization was not one of my strong suits.

Don Thorson from Chicago, a freshman in the foreign service school who already had been working with fellow young conservatives in the Midwest, was another key leader. Don was an excellent judge of people with a good instinct for what conservatives ought to do to advance our cause. Thorson and I have worked together on various political endeavors ever since we first hooked up at Georgetown as freshmen.

John Ryan and John Laytham came aboard the following year, with Ryan serving as our chief political operative while Laytham worked on attracting members to our organization. My role was to serve as the principal spokesman of our group as we did battle with the liberals.

However unlikely our prospects appeared to be in the beginning, somehow we succeeded in establishing a strong conservative presence on the Georgetown campus. Even the *Washington Post,* which idolized the Kennedy regime, expressed surprise at how influential among the students our Young Republican organization had become in such a short time.

We didn't pull any punches. Our Georgetown Young Republicans (YRs) were unapologetically conservative and openly critical of modern liberalism. Nor did we hesitate to publicly challenge Jesuit administrators and faculty members when we thought they were wrong. It seemed that the longer I remained at Georgetown the more politically liberal the Jesuits became.

During my time at Georgetown, the Jesuits were in the early stages of a radical transformation of a centuries-old religious order which had been founded in 1539 by Ignatius Loyola. The Jesuits I had known in high school were orthodox in their religious beliefs while generally apolitical. If they had strong political opinions, they seldom injected them into the classroom, particularly when it came to discussions of theology or philosophy.

At Georgetown things were different. I was suddenly confronted with a number of Jesuits like Father McSorley and others who argued in effect that in order to be a good Catholic, one had to be a liberal or leftist. McSorley taught a course in theology called Christian Social Justice, and it was nothing but pure, unvarnished left-wing politics.

The ideas of philosophers like Hegel and dissident Catholic theologians such as Teilhard de Chardin and Hans Kung came into vogue. The views of the Thomists (those who were considered followers of the great Catholic theologian Thomas Aquinas) were dismissed as antiquated at the new Georgetown.

Father Fitzgerald, who took over as dean of the College of Arts and Sciences during my latter years at Georgetown, signaled his opinion as to what intellectual direction he wanted the college to take by the prominent display of a picture of Teilhard de Chardin in his office. For those unfamiliar with the views of the controversial French theologian, Chardin thought that with the modern breakthroughs in the fields of science and technology mankind could construct a "heaven on earth" through a process of progressive advancement. His utopian vision contrasted sharply with the views of Augustine and Aquinas, who maintained that perfection would be attained only in the next world—Heaven.

"If men were angels" was a heresy that the framers of our Constitution had not succumbed to, as was made clear in *The Federalist*.

Seemingly out of nowhere, a French Jesuit who proclaimed that a perfect world (a heaven on earth) is within our potential became the "intellectual guru" for many at Georgetown, and the "progressive" priests in charge of the school turned the place upside down intellectually almost overnight in their rush to embrace this utopian vision.

What I didn't understand at the time was that the Jesuit community at Georgetown, itself was deeply divided. That explained the seeming contradiction between one resident theologian having us read books such as *Orthodoxy* by G. K. Chesterton and *The Drama of Atheist Humanism* by Fr. Henri de Lubac. Both of those works were classic defenses of Christianity. Meanwhile, another prominent theologian at Georgetown was preaching the "gospel" of Hans Kung, a dissident Catholic theologian who was highly critical of traditional Catholic thought. Increasingly, Georgetown became a university divided as to its core beliefs. College students were not the only members of our society profoundly affected by the turbulent winds of cultural change unleashed in the sixties.

On a separate front, the early sixties was a period in which there was an internecine political battle for control of the Republican party between what were known as the Rockefeller and Goldwater forces. Nixon's defeat at the hands of Kennedy in 1960 had left a power vacuum within the Republican structure that both liberal and conservative factions sought to fill. While the Rockefeller Republicans had substantial influence at the senior party level, both the Young Republicans and College Young Republicans tilted in the conservative direction. Due to the large number of young people who had become Republican activists by the early sixties, the voice of the young within the Republican party assumed influence in the 1964 presidential convention not seen before or since. The election of national officers at the biennial national conventions of the Young Republican National Federation and the College Republicans in the summer of 1963 was destined to have an inordinate impact on the Republican National Convention at San Francisco in 1964.

The Rockefeller forces began to sense the political danger of this influx of young conservatives into the GOP and belatedly tried to use organizational muscle and wads of money to woo young Republicans over to their side. They even funded a national magazine called *Advance* which was edited by Bruce Chapman (a leader of the Rockefeller youth forces who would later move to the right) in an attempt to combat the influence that *National Review* and other conservative publications were having on opinion leaders within Republican ranks.

With all the political money being tossed around by the Rockefeller crowd, the "pragmatic" course of action for budding young politicos would have been to join the Rockefeller forces. But most of us hung tough. We prided ourselves on the fact that our political principles weren't for sale. Conservatism wasn't a point of view we had adopted for convenience or to better our prospects for personal economic gain or to allow us to rub shoulders with prominent folks in the upper class who might be able to help us move up the career ladder after college.

The first College Young Republican regional convention I attended was in Virginia during the spring of 1962. We brought down a group of "green" conservatives from Georgetown to participate in the election of regional College Republican officers for the coming year. That particular College YR organization was then controlled by the Rockefeller forces. They couldn't have been nicer to us, the new kids on the block. Why, they even put us in charge of the platform committee, and we wrote a policy statement for the convention that Barry Goldwater would have been proud of. Our proposed platform passed overwhelmingly when presented to the convention delegates. Meanwhile, the Rockefeller forces stacked the credentials, rules, and nominations committee with a majority of their people. We were so naive at the time that we didn't realize that what they were doing practically ensured the election of their candidates to the various regional offices. So while we wound up with a wonderful platform which I am sure nobody ever bothered to read, the other side proceeded to elect all of its candidates to office and thus maintain control of the Region III College Young Republicans for one more year. We wouldn't make that mistake again.

By this time, outside of my studies and my job on Capitol Hill with Republican Congressman Bill Stinson from the state of Washington, most of my time was taken up with our efforts to advance the conservative movement. I had joined the college debate team my freshman year, but debating both sides of a single topic for an entire school year no longer held much appeal for me, and I figured that I already had benefited about as much as I ever would from the discipline of debating. My sophomore year, I ran for and was elected to the Georgetown student council. However, after I'd spent some time attending council meetings, student government issues seemed increasingly irrelevant. I was much more interested in the heated political debates taking place on campuses over such political issues as the Cuban missile crisis and our growing involvement in a ground war in Vietnam. So I decided to concentrate my energies on building a conservative movement on other campuses.

A steadily increasing number of young people identified themselves as "Goldwater Republicans." Our conservative populist movement was flourishing.

But the wave of political activism sweeping colleges was not limited to the Right. Our counterparts on the Left were also busy recruiting young supporters. Although no national political or intellectual figure emerged to energize and unite the Left as Goldwater and Buckley had done for the Right, a group of student radicals (who described themselves as New Leftists) were organizing their forces into a new national political movement. A number of them gathered at Port Huron, Michigan, in June 1962, and issued the Port Huron Statement. Drafted by Tom Hayden, it became the basic statement of principles for their organization, the Students for a Democratic Society (SDS).

Indeed, if any single individual could be identified as the principal leader of the New Left, it was Tom Hayden. While a student journalist at the University of Michigan in the late fifties, Hayden became involved in leftist politics. He aligned himself with a group of student radicals who took over the youth arm of a labor union organization known as the Student League for Industrial Democracy and converted it into the Students for a Democratic Society. SDS would emerge as the most influential organization of the New Left in the sixties and Hayden as its most effective leader. Hayden served in Atlanta as the first field secretary for SDS in 1961 where he first developed a reputation as a capable community organizer. But it was his authorship of the Port Huron Statement that thrust Hayden into a central leadership role with the emerging student radical movement.

In addition to Hayden, others present at that "founding" of the New Left (as described by Hayden in his autobiography *Reunion*) were: Paul Booth, a Swarthmore College student leader...Steve Max, whose father was a former editor of the U.S. Communist party newspaper, the *Daily Worker*...Dick and Mickey Flacks who were "descendants of the radical Jewish culture of New York City"...Al Haber, [whose] father was a senior university professor and official, a major figure in the Jewish community and a prominent national Democrat whose deep ties went back to his own youthful, New Deal idealism thirty years before...Sharon

Jeffrey, the daughter of Mildred Jeffrey, a top leader of the United Auto Workers, a close associate of Walter and Victor Reuther since the industrial strikes and sit-ins of the thirties, and a powerful woman in the Democratic party.

As Hayden and others have written, the gathering of student radicals at Port Huron led to the breakaway of the New Left from the traditional liberal wing of the Democratic party. Three years later SDS would divorce itself entirely from its parent organization, the League for Industrial Democracy, and become recognized as the leading New Left organization.

These fundamentally adversarial forces—the young conservatives and the New Leftists—later would lock horns over the issue of Vietnam. But, for now, both movements would focus most of their attention on building their own bases of political support. Conservatives concentrated on wresting control of the Republican party from the Eastern Establishment and its chief political leader, Governor Nelson Rockefeller of New York. Meanwhile, the New Left looked for a political issue with a broad enough appeal to attract massive numbers of young people to its side.

On the right, we believed that it was important to win control of the National Young Republican and College Republican organizations. Then, we would nominate Barry Goldwater as the Republican candidate for president in 1964 and take over the Republican party machinery.

I found myself in the middle of that intraparty contest.

The Rockefeller candidate for National College Republican chairman in 1963 was to be Ward White, a student at American University in Washington, D.C., who had been D.C. college chairman. The key leaders of the Goldwater movement within College YR ranks were Midwest College Republicans. They thought that, if they could elect a conservative to the D.C. college chairmanship, doing so would serve as a potentially crippling blow to White's candidacy for national CYR chairman. Thus, the election of the next D.C. college chairman became a major battleground between the Goldwater and Rockefeller camps.

I was the conservative candidate, and an unusually large number of delegates assembled at George Washington University in the spring of 1963 for the election. Our side was confident of victory going into the convention because our preliminary vote count indicated that I had the support of a majority of the delegates present.

We faced only one "minor" problem. The Rockefeller forces controlled the credentials committee which would certify those delegates who would be able to vote in the election. Using their control of this committee, the other side proceeded to declare a number of our delegates ineligible to vote, with the result that a majority of "certified" delegates now appeared to favor my opponent. When this decision of the credentials committee was announced, bedlam broke out in the hall. Many of our supporters were outraged and began yelling and screaming at the convention chairman, a Rockefeller Republican named Craig Distelhorst.

Of course, it didn't do our side any good to have some of our floor leaders lose their composure at a critical juncture in the battle. All the shouting in the world wasn't going to get the other side, which had control of the chair, to reverse the decision. It was clear that they were determined to elect their candidate one way or another. We had limited options—either figure out a way to get some of their supporters to switch sides or throw in the towel and concede defeat.

A transfer student at Georgetown University Business School whom I barely knew at the time, named John Ryan, saw what was happening and, without fanfare, assumed the role of our floor leader. He was an immediate calming influence on our forces. Ryan and I had already concluded that the opposition was not going to back down and reinstate our excluded delegates. So our only alternative was to switch some delegates who previously had committed to support my opponent. We didn't have much time, but John and I working together were able to swing some voters from the women's colleges, who had been offended by the tactics of the opposition, over to our side. It was a close election, but I won.

I learned two good political lessons from that unruly D.C. College YR convention in 1962. First, never give up until the final results are in—persistence and determination can turn defeat into victory. Also, when events go against you and you find yourself in a crisis environment, you learn a lot about the character and emotions of your friends and adversaries. In the scheme of things, this convention was a very small "pond," but to those of us in the midst of the battle, it was extremely important and we acted accordingly. That day at the convention, some individuals rose to the occasion and others panicked. Although we were young and politically naive at the time, our political principles stood us in good stead. I am convinced that we won some votes from delegates that day who may not have considered themselves Goldwater conservatives but admired the fact that we took our stand based on principle. We were idealists—young people involved in politics because we wanted to change the world for the better. I believe those feelings came across to other students who joined us and became part of this new conservative movement. While many Goldwater conservatives later would become cynical or disillusioned about the lofty ideals we professed, I remain convinced that our commitment to principle accounted for much of our success in attracting other young people to the conservative movement.

My election as the D.C. College Republican chairman allowed me to cast the deciding vote to elect the Goldwater candidate for national chairman at the College Republican National Convention in San Francisco in the summer of 1963.

A more important victory for the conservatives at that San Francisco convention, however, was the election of Goldwater supporter Donald E. Lukens to the chairmanship of the Young Republican National Federation. This was an important boost to the Draft Goldwater movement already underway. Those of us in the conservative camp were ecstatic. Conservatives were making tremendous headway in our efforts to take over the Republican party and nominate and elect Barry Goldwater the next president of the United States.

5

The End of Camelot

While we were busily engaged in trying to engineer a conservative takeover of the Republican party, the war in Indochina was beginning to emerge as a significant political issue within the United States.

On the Right, there was general support for American policy in Vietnam because opposition to the Marxist-Leninist ideology and the expansion of Communist power were central tenets of the conservative movement. However, most conservatives favored a tougher policy vis-á-vis the Communists than the containment strategy articulated by George Kennan, which then dominated State Department thinking. The Kennan approach favored policies which sought to limit and contain further Communist expansion. Truman had relied on the containment doctrine in defending South Korea from North Korean and Chinese Communist aggression. South Vietnam was the latest example of where the policy of containment was being utilized to prevent Communist expansionism.

Many of us within conservative ranks found this purely defensive foreign policy strategy repugnant and considered Kennan's containment policy analogous to requiring your football team to play on defense for the entire game. If the best you can hope for is the preservation of the status quo, the odds are that you are going to suffer occasional setbacks in certain regions of the world, with the result that more peoples and more territories likely would fall under Communist influence. I gave many a speech to college audiences in the sixties, arguing that such a strategy was a slow, but sure road to international defeat in our ongoing struggle against Communism.

Our objective was the liberation of peoples and nations who were under Communist domination, whether in North Vietnam, Eastern Europe, Cuba, or elsewhere. But it was the Cuban issue, not the war in Vietnam, that dominated the headlines and the foreign policy debate in the early sixties. The Right wanted Castro overthrown. The memory of the failed Bay of Pigs invasion in 1961 and the Soviet introduction of offensive missiles in Cuba one year later added fuel to the conservative demands for Castro's ouster.

In contrast, New Leftists portrayed Fidel Castro and his revolutionary sidekick Che Guevara as cult heroes who were models for a new style of socialist leadership in the western hemisphere. As Tom Hayden acknowledged in his autobiography, New Left leaders in the United States had a tendency to romanticize real revolutionaries like Che Guevara: "Many, including myself, were inspired by the romantic guerrilla adventures of Che Guevara in Latin America."

Gradually, however, the principal foreign policy debate on campus shifted from Fidel Castro to the growing war in Indochina.

At Georgetown, the Philodemic Society encouraged debates among student members on prominent issues of the day. Although no longer involved on the debate team, I was active in the Philodemic Society and enjoyed participating in the various debates held under its auspices.

In 1962 Ambassador Averell Harriman negotiated the Laotian Accords on behalf of the Kennedy administration. The accords basically ceded the country of Laos to the Communist Pathet Lao forces. The question of the day before the Philodemic Society was whether this was a wise decision in terms of the effect it would have on Indochina. In the debate I took the negative, arguing that the Harriman accords effectively turned control of that country over to the Communists and jeopardized our ability to wage war in Indochina.

The main supporter of the resolution was Bob Shrum. Bob and I had first met as we walked down to the gym to register for our freshman classes. We lived near each other on the third floor of a dorm known as New North. Bob was a brilliant student from California who went on to become a national collegiate debate champion. He was a dedicated liberal who was excited about the Kennedys coming to power. We got into a political argument on our way down to freshman class registration, and we continued disagreeing throughout our time together at Georgetown. That didn't stop us from liking one another.

Shrum maintained in the debate that the situation was virtually hopeless in Laos, that pro-Western forces in that country were headed for certain defeat anyway, and that a negotiated settlement with the Communists was the best deal we could hope to cut under such adverse circumstances. By effectively ceding Laos to the Communists, Shrum argued, we could refocus our energy and resources on the major threat to the region—the attempted Communist takeover of South Vietnam. In South Vietnam we had a far more favorable situation, militarily and politically. The South Vietnamese government of President Ngo Dinh Diem was stronger and far more stable than its pro-Western counterpart in Laos. Shrum argued that Vietnam was where we should make our stand in Southeast Asia. There, he said, we could fight and win.

Bob Shrum's viewpoint prevailed in the halls of the Philodemic Society that day as a majority of those present voted in favor of the proposition that the Harriman accords were in the best interest of American policy in Southeast Asia.

Within months of our debate over the Harriman accords, the attitude of American opinion makers toward the Diem government in South Vietnam began to shift. Previously, liberals and conservatives alike had been supportive of President Diem. Liberal Supreme Court Justice William O. Douglas had even referred to

Diem years earlier in glowing terms: "Ngo Dinh Diem is revered by the Vietnamese because he is honest and independent and stood firm against the French influence."

But certain American journalists covering the war, such as David Halberstam and Malcolm Browne, had a more negative view of the Diem government. These two young reporters were fast making a name for themselves with their sensationalist stories about Buddhist dissent in South Vietnam. In fact, most American reporters who were writing for such influential media outlets as the *New York Times* and the Associated Press were uniformly hostile to the Diem regime while sympathizing with the Buddhist dissident movement in Saigon and Hue.

The drumbeats began both in the press corps and within certain circles of the Kennedy administration for the replacement of the Diem government by a more "progressive and democratic" regime in the South. A new government supposedly would be more able to rally all elements of Vietnamese society, particularly the Buddhist majority, behind the prosecution of the war against the Viet Cong and North Vietnamese Communists. Averell Harriman, undersecretary of state for political affairs, Roger Hilsman, assistant secretary of state for Far Eastern Affairs, and Arthur Schlesinger, Jr., a White House adviser, led the way in trying to push President Kennedy into "dumping" Diem.

What we as students, attempting to follow the confusing political situation through dispatches filed by American reporters from Vietnam, didn't know at the time, was that South Vietnamese and American conspirators already were plotting to overthrow Diem and replace him with a military junta.

One of the few journalistic voices raised in opposition to the growing demand for Diem's ouster was that of Marguerite Higgins, a reporter for the *New York Herald-Tribune*. She had had many years of experience covering the political and military situation in the Far East.

Higgins was appalled at the attitude of the new American Ambassador Henry Cabot Lodge as well as various State Department officials who were no longer even bothering to disguise their view that Diem had to go because of the highly publicized opposition to his regime by militant Buddhist sects.

In her book *Our Vietnam Nightmare,* Higgins recounts one conversation she had on this subject with a State Department official and a comment made by Roger Hilsman:

> In Washington,... one official asked me plaintively: "Don't you realize that Diem is tarnishing our image everywhere in the world?"
>
> "But," I countered, "if the United States were to state the facts—that this is a political, not a religious matter—wouldn't that in itself help to put the matter in perspective and help everybody's image?"
>
> "The rights and wrongs don't matter," said the official, "it's what people believe."
>
> Or as Roger Hilsman, Assistant Secretary of State for Far Eastern affairs put it (in a talk with Hearst's Frank Coniff), "After the closing of the pagodas on August 21, the facts became irrelevant."

Ms. Higgins soon learned that these and other comments made by Kennedy administration officials effectively meant that Diem was on his way out: "I did not realize how far the disassociation [of the Kennedy Administration from President Diem] was to go until Friday, August 23, when an old friend at the Department of State told me that 'Diem will be overthrown in a matter of days.'"

While supporters of the war effort quarreled over whether Diem should stay or go, the leaders of the New Left were quite open in expressing their hope for a Viet Cong victory. From their perspective, Diem or any of his likely successors were simply puppets of the American colonialists who sought domination of South Vietnam for purposes of economic exploitation. Thus, it didn't make any difference to the Left who took over from Diem unless the changes led to the formation of a coalition government which included the Viet Cong in the sharing of power.

While the views of the New Left were considered very extreme in this 1962-63 time frame (even on college campuses), the constant barrage of criticism of the Diem regime from liberal and leftist circles had the desired effect of creating doubts among the American public about U.S. support of his government. In particular, the media was very critical of Diem's brother and close adviser Ngo Dinh Nhu, along with Nhu's controversial wife, Madame Ngo Dinh Nhu (who was referred to in the American media as the "Dragon Lady").

In order to rebut or neutralize the negative publicity the Diem family was receiving in the United States, either on her own or upon the suggestion of her advisers, Madame Nhu decided to embark on a speaking tour in the United States to counter the image she had in America and to try to convey to the American public the positive side of her brother-in-law's government. She spoke on a number of college campuses, including Georgetown University.

At Georgetown she received a cordial, although not particularly enthusiastic, reception. At most of the other universities she visited, Madame Nhu was greeted by hostile audiences. If anything, her trip served only to further darken her reputation among Americans who knew very little about the Diem family or political factionalism in South Vietnam. Madame Nhu's speaking tour turned out to be a public relations disaster which provided the Left with additional ammunition in its immediate goal of getting rid of the Diem government.

Those of us involved in the campus debates, which were beginning to heat up over the war in Vietnam, did not expect at the time of Madame Nhu's visit to the United States that her brother-in-law, President Diem, would be overthrown a few months later in a military coup that had the covert backing of the Kennedy administration.

The procoup faction of Lodge, Harriman, Hilsman, et al., within the Kennedy Administration had gained the upper hand and "encouraged" Vietnamese military commanders to lead a revolt to topple Diem. Vietnamese coup leaders included Gen. Duong Van (Big) Minh, the leader of the first junta to take power after Diem's overthrow; Gen. Tran Thien Khiem, the army chief of staff; Army Commander Tran Van Don; Maj. Gen. Mai Huu Xuan; and Nguyen Ngoc Tho, the Vietnamese vice president.

Once the coup began, President Diem and his brother went into hiding. He then attempted to seek refuge in the U.S. Embassy, but was turned away by Ambassador Henry Cabot Lodge. Then, upon promise of safe conduct out of the country to a place of exile of his choosing, Diem agreed to turn himself over to the army. Instead of receiving safe conduct, the president and his brother were executed on orders of the coup leaders. As General Minh later said, "Diem could not be allowed to live because he was too much respected among simple, gullible people in the countryside, especially the Catholics and the refugees. We had to kill Nhu [Diem's brother] because he was so widely feared—and he had created organizations that were arms of his personal power."

After President Diem had been overthrown and assassinated in the American-assisted military coup in 1963, succeeding governments in South Vietnam had found it difficult to reestablish a strong political infrastructure capable of dealing with the highly disciplined and unified Viet Cong infrastructure.

Duong Van Minh, "Big Minh," and other coup leaders would themselves be ousted from power within a year by Gen. Nguyen Khan, and the musical-chair succession of regimes in the South would continue until General Thieu came to power in 1967.

Whatever his faults, Diem had been a nationalist leader who had pulled South Vietnam together in the fifties when it appeared that it would be only a matter of time before Ho Chi Minh and the Communist government of North Vietnam controlled the entire country. Diem developed an effective governmental infrastructure which was broken up when the military coup leaders took over in 1963. Thereafter, control of the government in South Vietnam became something akin to a revolving door of political and military leaders attempting to consolidate power in the South. I saw the effects of this constant struggle for political power in South Vietnam in the factionalism within various segments of the Vietnamese community in the Delta during my own tour of duty years later.

The Vietnamese I worked with and got to know didn't want to live under Communism, but they couldn't agree on how to work together to win the war. Thus, even in 1969 under President Thieu, the political infrastructure of the South Vietnamese government was weaker than it had been under President Diem. In fact, many Vietnamese were nostalgic about the days of Diem, leading me to wonder if President Diem might not have returned to power had he been sent into exile in 1963 rather than assassinated.

Diem's downfall had been fueled by militant Buddhist-led opposition to his regime. This so-called religious conflict between a Catholic president in the person of Diem and certain segments of the Buddhist community had been highly publicized by reporters for the *New York Times* and other prestigious publications who openly advocated the replacement of President Diem by some other leader who could garner the full support of the Buddhist majority.

I never imagined at the time that the U.S.-authorized overthrow of the Diem government would be the catalyst leading to a deepening American involvement in the war—one that would have such an impact upon my generation. At the time of Diem's death, there were only 17,000 American military advisers in Vietnam. The stated objective of American policy then was to play a supporting role in the South Vietnamese government's campaign to defeat the Communist insurgency. Thereafter, incrementally, the war in Vietnam became more and more an American-directed enterprise. And that meant more Americans would be needed to fight that war.

As much as conservatives were dismayed over events in South Vietnam, our attention was riveted on winning the Republican nomination for Barry Goldwater and on defeating John Kennedy in the 1964 presidential election. After Goldwater's election, we assumed he would put an end, somehow, to the Communist threat to take over South Vietnam.

Suddenly, the idea of a conservative like Barry Goldwater being elected president didn't seem so crazy. We were riding high. This essentially middle-class political revolution was on the threshold of capturing the Republican party and running a competitive race for the presidency of the United States.

What a different kind of Republican party it would be with these young conservatives taking control. Many of us never would have joined the party of Willkie, Dewey, Scranton, and Rockefeller, which was so closely identified with big business and Wall Street interests. Nor did we have much respect for upper-class society types (or those trying to buy or wheedle their way into such circles) who were Republicans by birth or Republicans for class reasons. We had left the majority party to become Republicans because of a commitment to conservative values. Not only was our political philosophy at odds with the pragmatism of the Eastern-based leadership of the party, most of us were middle-class to the core. Many of our leaders were offspring of traditionally Democratic families who grew up in Democratic party strongholds like Chicago and New York or the still solidly Democratic South. A high percentage of us were "ethnics," products of backgrounds normally associated with Democratic politics, such as Irish, Italian, and Polish. There was also a great influx of Catholics and Southern fundamentalist Protestants into Republican ranks. People like Brian Whalen and Alan Drazek from Chicago, Gary Fairchild from Wheaton College, David Keene and John Savage from Wisconsin, Ken Tomlinson from Virginia, Jim Sensenbrenner from Stanford, along with Morton Blackwell and Rob Pollock from Louisiana, were just a few of the student leaders attracted to the Republican party because of this new populist brand of conservatism being preached by Barry Goldwater. Even among members of the Jewish faith, a religious group solidly wedded to the Democratic party since the days of Franklin Roosevelt, there were faint stirrings of movement from children of disillusioned old leftists, young libertarian economists, and committed anti-Communists.

It was an eclectic collection of individualists who came together on the right in the early sixties. We shared a strong sense of loyalty to conservative principles and to one another. For a while, it even looked as though we might be able to do the impossible and drive the Liberal Establishment from power.

Then everything fell apart. A single event—the assassination of John F. Kennedy by Lee Harvey Oswald in my hometown of Dallas on November 23, 1963—had as catastrophic an impact on the conservative movement as it did on the larger society.

A new Democratic president from Texas, Lyndon Johnson, pulled Texans back into the Democratic column. Around the country the new conservative movement stalled before going into a decline. It didn't disappear overnight, but slow attrition combined with the dramatic political reversals of 1964 would take its toll.

How ironic it was that a leftist, Lee Harvey Oswald, would kill a liberal president, and, in so doing, achieve the side effect of seriously wounding a conservative movement that was providing the most vigorous opposition to the Left that the country had seen.

Still there was enough steam left in the conservative movement to capture the 1964 Republican presidential nomination for Barry Goldwater. But Goldwater vs. Johnson just wasn't the same as Goldwater vs. Kennedy would have been. In retrospect, no one could have beaten the man who rhetorically was "carrying forth the programs of our fallen leader."

Lyndon Johnson "inherited" the office of the presidency with the sympathy of an electorate ready to circle the wagons around their new president while trying to recover from the shock of the assassination of John F. Kennedy. One way to aid in that recovery was to return the "fallen leader's successor" to the White House.

I worked throughout the 1964 campaign at Goldwater headquarters in Washington, D.C. I had gotten the job through the recommendation of my good friend and fellow Georgetown conservative Don Thorson. I was in the research division under the late Frank R. Lee, who was the press secretary at the time for Senator Peter Dominick, a leading conservative from Colorado.

Frank and I became fast friends, and neither of us harbored any illusions that Goldwater stood a chance of winning the November election. As part of our opposition research efforts, we became very familiar with Lyndon Johnson's questionable political and business dealings over the years, from the stuffing of the ballot box in his eighty-seven vote 1948 "victory" over Coke Stevenson to his use of his position in Congress to build a broadcasting empire that made him a multimillionaire. But the press was not interested in LBJ's abuse of power—at that time. They dismissed out of hand the examples of LBJ's illegitimate use of power recounted by Texas historian J. Evetts Haley in *A Texan Looks at Lyndon*. It would take another historian from the East, Robert Caro, to confirm much of what Haley had to say about LBJ, some twenty-five years later.

The media was instead obsessed with Barry Goldwater's "extremism." Goldwater gave his adversaries the ammunition they were looking for when he stated in his acceptance speech after his nomination at the Republican National Convention in

San Francisco that "Extremism in the defense of liberty is no vice, moderation in the pursuit of justice is no virtue."

The Johnson campaign exploited this image of Goldwater as a dangerous "extremist" by running slick television ads such as one with a little girl picking flowers who is interrupted by a nuclear explosion. The message of the Johnson media campaign orchestrated by Bill Moyers was one that blatantly appealed to the fear factor—that the election of Barry Goldwater would get us into a nuclear war. Other ads suggested that Goldwater was going to take away the social security checks of the elderly.

The emotional appeals worked. Before long, it was obvious to all but the most fanatical Goldwater supporters that we were heading for a major defeat. Already, some of us within the conservative movement were beginning to speculate on what we should do to rally our forces after the election. Don Thorson came up with the best idea: get behind Sen. Peter Dominick and encourage him to run. Frank Lee was getting firsthand experience in a presidential campaign, and that could prove very valuable if Dominick were to make a future bid for the Presidency. We didn't see any other viable candidate at the time as the next political leader of the conservative movement.

But that was before Ronald Reagan's stirring thirty-minute television address that fall. This "movie actor from Hollywood" articulated the conservative vision of what he called "the shining city on the hill" far more effectively than anything else the campaign had produced.

Although I didn't know it at the time, apparently there was a serious disagreement at the highest levels of the Goldwater campaign whether to air the Reagan speech. But, his address appeared on national television, and that single event helped to change American history. Overnight, Ronald Reagan became the heir-apparent to Goldwater as the political leader of the conservative movement even though he was dismissed by most opinion leaders as just "an actor reading a script."

The national election was even worse than we had anticipated. The Johnson landslide led to the defeat of many excellent Republican candidates running for state and national offices. Voters abandoned the Republican party in droves.

After the election, I had the unpleasant assignment at the Republican National Committee of having to phone Republican officials throughout the country to get confirmation of the election results in their localities and states. I was a handy target as a committee staff member for them to blow off a lot of pent-up anger. And they sure did. Time and time again I was told that this was the worst defeat that the Republican party had ever suffered in their lifetime, and they didn't know if the party would be able to recover.

I can't say that I was much more optimistic about our future than many of the leaders around the country with whom I had spoken. It was as if we were starting all over again.

In the wake of the Johnson landslide, our formerly unified conservative movement split into various political factions. Some conservatives became "pragmatic": convinced that a real conservative could never be elected president of the United States and that the best we could expect would be to elect a middle-of-the-road Republican like Richard Nixon.

A second group within the conservative movement took the opposite tack, becoming even more ideologically rigid than before. Perhaps these folks subconsciously reconciled themselves to the notion that they were fighting a losing battle, but one that they were determined to carry on anyway. I refer to this group as "kamikaze right-wingers." In their hearts, they didn't believe that we had a chance of winning, so they were going to go down to political defeat with "guns blazing."

Still other conservatives just quit the movement or drifted away, saying "to hell with politics, I'll just concentrate on making money."

It was not a pretty sight from the conservative vantage point as old friends within the movement now found themselves on opposite sides in internal Republican party disputes. A once powerful political force was in a shambles.

Even with Goldwater's defeat, conservatives still controlled the machinery of their party. But that wouldn't last for long at the senior party level. Dean Burch, the Goldwater campaign leader whom Goldwater had named party chairman, resigned and was replaced by a professional political technician from Ohio named Ray Bliss, who was basically a nonideological Republican.

Conservatives still had control of the Young Republican and College Young Republican national organizations. At the 1965 national YR and CYR conventions, conservatives elected Tom Van Sickle as YR national chairman, and I was elected CYR national chairman. As an indication of how much conservative influence there was within College Republican ranks, I ran unopposed.

However, Ray Bliss wasn't pleased with my election. He wanted a more "controllable" and less ideological campus Republican organization. So he cut off our money and also hired a liberal Republican professor to set up a separate college outreach effort. Bliss later added Howard Phillips (now associated with the New Right, he was then a liberal Massachusetts Republican) to his staff, apparently with the idea of trying to establish a competing student Republican organization to our College Republican National Committee.

None of this particularly bothered us. We went out and raised our own money. One of Bill Buckley's associates at *National Review,* Neal Freeman, drafted an effective fundraising letter for our College Republican organization and conservative activists around the country contributed sufficient funds to allow us to maintain our independence and function effectively. Plus, I served practically full-time as an unpaid chairman while taking graduate studies in political science at Georgetown.

6

Vietnam and the Rise
of the New Left

By the fall of 1965, as College Republican chairman, I was speaking and debating on campuses all over the country. More and more, the war in Vietnam became the paramount issue of concern to college audiences. By then, the American troop buildup had begun in earnest, and U.S. combat units were now fighting in Vietnam. Most conservatives were still committed to a policy of defeating Communism in South Vietnam, but the war had dragged on longer than most Americans were willing to accept, and there seemed to be no quick end in sight. The "protracted war" in Vietnam finally gave the New Left the opportunity to gain a major foothold on our college campuses.

Their previous efforts to rally students around the so-called free speech movement which erupted at the Berkeley campus of the University of California in the early sixties and to take over control and direction of the popular civil rights movement, had ended in failure. But Vietnam was "made to order" for the New Left. On college campuses throughout the country, young males were at risk of being drafted and sent off to Vietnam where other young Americans were dying in steadily increasing numbers.

So the New Left provided political ammunition through speeches, writings, campus teach-ins, and organized protests against the war—helping draft-aged young men justify their personal desire to avoid military service in general and Vietnam in particular. New Left leaders correctly sensed that this single issue had the potential to radicalize a significant number of young Americans from the sixties generation. This new breed of student radicals wasn't just against the war in Vietnam. They were on the other side.

My first major exposure to the national dimensions of this new political phenomenon came in 1965 when I observed a major demonstration against the war in Washington organized by the Students for a Democratic Society (SDS). The chants "Hey, hey, LBJ, how many kids did you kill today?" and "Ho, Ho, Ho Chi Minh," the flurry of Viet Cong flags being carried by the demonstrators, the signs referring to American soldiers in Vietnam as "baby killers," and the speech-making by a variety of radical activists, all added up to a clear message: America is supporting the wrong side in that war. We will do what we can to see that America and our South Vietnamese allies go down to defeat in Vietnam.

Walking away from the crowd that afternoon, I couldn't help but be impressed by the formidable political movement SDS had mobilized in the three years since the Port Huron Statement. This was a movement to be reckoned with. What also took me by surprise that hot, summer day in Washington was the degree of contempt the New Leftists had for the old Liberal Establishment.

Clark Kissinger, the executive secretary of SDS, denounced liberals as "guardians of the corporate state." His comments were wildly applauded. Thus, another group was attacking Establishment liberalism just as forcefully from the Left as the young conservatives were attacking it from the Right. The lines were being drawn on both sides of the political aisle for a later confrontation between conservative populism and Leftist populism, although at the time the Liberal Establishment seemed to be the principal target of both sides.

But, at the time, most American students still supported the goal of defeating the Communist attempt to take over South

Vietnam. Even with protest rallies that were drawing bigger and bigger crowds, leftist support among the young had yet to match, either in terms of number of followers or impact on the campuses, that of our movement. When I was national chairman of the College Republicans, we had approximately eight hundred chapters on college campuses and over 110,000 members. We were the largest student political organization in America at the time.

But the political momentum was beginning to turn against us. SDS and other anti-Vietnam organizations were gaining in influence on the campuses, aided to no small degree by the support of university professors and journalists sympathetic to their cause.

While the political momentum was beginning to shift on the war issue, there was still a lot of support on the campuses for our soldiers in Vietnam. As a way of proving that point, in the fall of 1965 I organized a bipartisan National Student Committee for the Defense of Vietnam.

Our initial press conference was on the campus of Georgetown University's School of Foreign Service. A throng of reporters turned out for the event where we announced a national petition drive on campuses across the country in support of our troops in Vietnam. After the three of us on the stage made our opening statements, we turned it over to the press for questions.

The only question I still remember was the one raised by a young journalist from *U.S. News & World Report* who wanted to know what our current draft status was and what our own plans were regarding military service. I assumed he was trying to make the point that none of us on the stage seemed to be in a hurry to sign up for Vietnam. I was prepared for that particular question although my colleagues on the podium appeared taken aback. I had been wrestling with what I was going to do about military service for some time. Being of draft age myself, would I join the military or rely indefinitely on a student deferment in order to avoid military service? It was a fair question, even though I thought the young reporter in his bow tie and seersucker suit was a wise ass trying to embarrass us.

I knew in my mind that I would be nothing but a hypocrite if I ducked my own obligation to serve. So the reporter's question gave me the opportunity to declare publicly what I had already made up my mind to do—I would enlist in the military once my term as College Republican chairman was completed.

I was tempted to ask the young reporter what his own military status was, but decided that it was better to keep my mouth shut and play it straight.

A few of us worked long hours over the next few months to coordinate this national petition campaign. Our goal was to produce hard evidence that the New Left's views on Vietnam were unrepresentative of the opinions of the student population at large. We were more successful than we had anticipated.

By January, 1966, we had identified and collected signatures from more than half a million students on more than three hundred campuses across the country. This was accomplished on a budget of practically zero, with the only substantial contributions received being the use of long distance WATS lines that enabled us to contact student leaders all over America who were working on the project with us.

Next came my first, direct exposure to the Washington policy makers who were directing the war effort in Vietnam. I wanted to set up a meeting with the president, to present the petition, figuring that the Johnson administration would be eager to meet with any student group supporting American policy in Vietnam, particularly in light of the large number of student signatures we had collected.

I met first with an official on McGeorge Bundy's staff at the National Security Council, whose job included encouraging domestic support for administration policy in Vietnam. He was vague about setting up a meeting with Lyndon Johnson. I had the feeling that he didn't quite know what to do with our group. I could only guess that he was afraid, since I was a campus leader of the Republican party, my views on Vietnam were probably closer to Barry Goldwater's than to the current Johnson-McNamara-Bundy policy of prosecuting the war. He was, of course, correct. But I tried to convince him that all we wanted to do was to counteract the growing impression from the New Left that most college students were opposed to our being in Vietnam. Finally, he decided to solve a potential problem by having us make our presentation to Vice President Humphrey instead.

We met in the vice president's office with what seemed like most of the White House press corps in attendance. Hubert Humphrey couldn't have been nicer to us although he seemed to talk on endlessly, living up to his loquacious reputation. After we finished our presentation, we were peppered with questions. What took me aback was the hostility from many of the journalists in the room. A few reporters tried to poke holes in the results of our petition campaign, while the *New York Times* reporter implied that we had made up our figures. These weren't members of the "alternative" press, but representatives of the most prestigious newspapers in America, including the *Washington Post.*

We had done our homework, however, and provided the reporters with whatever back-up data they requested. A few made it very clear that they just didn't believe that half a million American college students still supported our soldiers in Vietnam.

I left that day proud of what we had accomplished in a matter of just a few months. By this point in the war, conservatives were providing the only real leadership on the campuses for the proposition that we should defend South Vietnam against Communist aggression. Most Young Democratic organizations held views on Vietnam closer to those of the New Left than their own Democratic administration. Additionally, my initial exposure to leading members of the Washington press corps led me to conclude that the mainstream press had turned against the war.

What I didn't realize at the time was that the Liberal Establishment policy makers like Robert McNamara, McGeorge Bundy, Roger Hilsman, and others, who were directing our strategy in Vietnam, were in the process of changing their minds about the efficacy of defeating Communism in South Vietnam.

In January, 1966, I still believed that our side would prevail. However, the mood was growing ugly on the campuses. Debates over the war became more acrimonious, with leftist activists using obscenities to shout down speakers like me who sought to defend American objectives in Vietnam. Emotion displaced reason and student radicals correctly sensed that their ability to effectively shut down real debate on the issue at various universities across the country worked to their advantage in their efforts to mobilize political support. I had more than a few unpleasant experiences trying to articulate a dissenting view to the leftist line on Vietnam. One time when I was speaking at a campus teach-in, a radical type came running down the aisle shouting obscenities in an obvious attempt to disrupt my presentation.

The media's attitude toward the New Left was frustrating to those of us on the other side of the Vietnam debate who saw the student radicals up close. So many of the leftist "celebrities" struck me as little more than ego-tripping media hounds whose influence on the campuses was vastly overestimated. I never was particularly concerned that well-publicized radicals such as Jerry Rubin or Abbie Hoffman would be able to usher in dramatic changes in the American political system. We viewed Rubin and Hoffman as leftist clowns trying to draw attention to themselves by acting out a series of outrageous stunts designed to shock middle-class America.

Yet the New Left had its share of serious-minded leaders who knew exactly what they were doing in their attempts to advance the "revolutionary agenda."

Tom Hayden was one such leader as I discovered for myself one evening at Fairleigh Dickinson University in New Jersey at an all-night teach-in on the Vietnam issue. All shades of opinion were represented by the speakers who addressed the students during the course of the evening. I participated, along with Democratic Senator Birch Bayh from Indiana, conservative newsman Fulton Lewis III, Hayden, and others.

One of the spokesmen for the Left was a self-proclaimed Marxist who took what I viewed as the Stalinist position on the war: Ho Chi Minh and the North Vietnamese Communists were a progressive group of nationalists fighting against the American "imperialists" and their South Vietnamese "puppet" regime.

Tom Hayden offered a more sophisticated rationale as to why the United States and our South Vietnamese allies should lose the war. He argued that the Viet Cong, the South Vietnamese arm of the Communist forces in Indochina, truly represented the sentiments of the South Vietnamese people and would establish a more equitable regime if allowed to come to power.

Listening to Hayden speak that evening, it didn't take me long to figure out that this guy was no Abbie Hoffman or Jerry Rubin.

He came across as an intensely brilliant firebrand, who had a look in his eyes which suggested that he would not hesitate to trample anyone who got in the way of the "revolution." A later, favorable article in the *Village Voice* said that Hayden saw himself as the Ho Chi Minh of America. I didn't doubt it after watching him in action that evening. This guy was serious about making a political revolution in America, and he had a strategic sense of how the Left could accomplish that goal. As a political issue, Vietnam was the perfect ideological weapon for Hayden to use as he sought to mobilize large masses of young people against the American political system.

As was the case with most of the Vietnam teach-ins being held on college campuses in those days, those of us on the conservative side of the debate were underrepresented that evening. (In some teach-ins, those who supported the principle of defeating Communism in South Vietnam weren't even allowed to participate.)

Fulton Lewis III, the son of the famous radio commentator for Mutual Radio, Fulton Lewis, Jr., and I were the two principal speakers for the conservatives. I tried to make the point in my remarks that the Viet Cong were effectively under the control of Ho Chi Minh's regime. Many Vietnamese already had declared their position on living under a Communist regime in the North by voting with their feet and fleeing to South Vietnam in the mid-fifties when they were given the opportunity. Clearly, I argued, the people of South Vietnam did not want to live under Communism. The battle for South Vietnam was not a choice between an indigenous, progressive group of guerrillas vs. a right-wing dictatorship but was a struggle between a hardened Communist regime in North Vietnam and a society in the South that wanted to maintain independence from Communist rule.

As so often happened when I debated the Vietnam issue on college campuses, New Left types in the audience attempted to shout me down while I was speaking. But I was used to the drill by then, and resumed my remarks once the shouting had died down. Student radicals were not known for their willingness to listen to anyone who disagreed with them. I left the event that evening pleased with the overall reception I had received. At least I had offered the students a different perspective on the war than they were accustomed to hearing from their liberal professors and resident campus radicals.

When it came to the question of American policy toward Vietnam, about the only effective opposition to the New Left was coming from the conservatives. New Deal and New Frontier liberals didn't know how to deal with this new breed of leftists except to cave in to their demands. And political pragmatists were unable to come to grips with, and effectively respond to, the so-called idealism of the student radicals. We conservatives were not intimidated by the New Left.

There was little in common between the new conservatives and the student radicals other than a mutual disenchantment with the policies of the Liberal Establishment. Neither movement had any use for Secretary of Defense Robert McNamara, whom both sides viewed as the principal architect of our Vietnam policy. To the Left, McNamara was a "war criminal" while the Right saw him as a "corporate technocrat" whose policy of gradual escalation of the war in order to bring the North Vietnamese government to the negotiating table was a "no-win" strategy.

Not only were young conservatives and New Leftists political opposites, we were temperamentally dissimilar. Traditionally-oriented families tended to produce conservative activists, whereas, when it came to the Left, the trend was *Liberal Parents, Radical Children,* to use the title of a book by Midge Dector.

While the conservative movement was middle class to the core, New Left leaders tended to be products of upper-middle class, liberal households. Whereas the young conservatives by and large were religious believers, the Left was heavily populated with ex-Catholics, secularized Jews, and humanistic Protestants, who either no longer believed in God or favored a watered-down, World Council of Churches kind of religion which emphasized "social justice" issues rather than salvation. For example, SDS leader Tom Hayden was an ex-Catholic and a religious nonbeliever.

By and large, the student radicals viewed religion as useful only insofar as the churches helped further the goal of building a heaven on earth (a humane Marxism, if you will) under New Left auspices.

Educationally, their ranks included a high percentage of graduate students and teaching assistants, particularly in such fields as political science, history, English, economics, and philosophy. They were apt to be found in the most prestigious universities with more liberal reputations, such as the University of California at Berkeley, the University of Michigan, Columbia University, the University of Wisconsin, and the Ivy League schools. (Interestingly enough, the New Left seemed to have only a minimum impact on colleges in the Sunbelt—excluding some California schools—at Catholic universities, and at fundamentalist Christian colleges like Wheaton in Illinois).

In *Roots of Radicalism,* Professors Stanley Rothman and Robert Lichter have described the backgrounds and value systems of the families who produced many of the SDS leaders:

> Their fathers were mostly wealthy, well-educated, upper middle-class professionals, such as college faculty, doctors, and lawyers. Their parents were politically liberal and also shared the socially liberal values of intellectualism, estheticism, secularism and self-expression.

By late 1966 and early 1967, the tide was clearly shifting in favor of the New Left as it began to displace the College Republicans as the most influential political force on the campuses. In fact, by 1968 SDS claimed some eighty to a hundred thousand recruits on several hundred campuses.

My own university was becoming virtually unrecognizable. Contemporaneous with the growing influence at Georgetown of the so-called progressive faction of Jesuits, a number of students were clamoring for change. While I was still an undergraduate, a group of us got into a heated discussion one day about what kind of university Georgetown ought to be. Two of my classmates (Bob Shrum and Phil Vasta), both of whom later would go on to Harvard for graduate studies, argued that Georgetown should try to become more like the Ivy League schools.

How was this to be accomplished? By not being so "parochial," which meant in their parlance that Georgetown should be less Catholic in its values, and by deemphasizing traditional philosophy and theology along with an approach that values education for its own sake. Instead, make Georgetown more "relevant" by adding new departments of sociology and psychology while stressing a behaviorist approach to human knowledge.

Simply put, my classmates' objective was to turn Georgetown University into a secular institution modeled after schools such as Harvard and Yale.

In our debate over the future direction of Georgetown, I argued that the university should maintain its unique character—one clearly distinct from that of the Ivy League schools or state universities. My two opponents, both of whom were highly intelligent and very articulate, told me that their position ultimately would prevail and that Georgetown would join the ranks one day of the elite Ivy League institutions in our country. I sensed at the time that they were probably right. I just didn't think the changes would come so quickly.

Bill Clinton's freshman year in Georgetown University's School of Foreign Service was 1965. We became acquainted as a result of our mutual interest in politics. Within a short time after his arrival, he was elected president of his freshman class and was being spoken of even then as a young man with a bright political future. At the time, Clinton didn't appear to be caught up in the New Left movement. He styled himself a Kennedy Democrat and struck me as the "corporate liberal" type of young politico—intent on moving up the political ladder as rapidly as possible and willing to adjust his views accordingly in order to succeed.

Georgetown University in 1965 was not yet a hotbed of leftist politics. There were few, if any, students from our school who participated that summer in the SDS demonstration against the war in Washington, D.C. Thus, it was surprising when I later learned that Clinton had turned to the left politically in the late sixties and joined the anti-Vietnam protest movement.

In retrospect, however, that political shift of Bill Clinton to the left in the latter part of that decade becomes more explainable. By the mid-sixties, the mood on college campuses was changing. As the war heated up and an increasing number of young men were dying in Vietnam, draft-aged students were more susceptible to the New Left's position that America was the villain in Vietnam. Apparently, Bill Clinton bought the student radical line concerning the war and became a full-fledged member of the anti-Vietnam protest movement while at Georgetown and continued his active participation thereafter as a Rhodes scholar at Oxford in 1969.

The "new Georgetown" fell into step with the conventional wisdom of the leftist academics that America was engaged in an immoral war. Professor George Carey was one of the few professors at Georgetown who dared to dissent publicly from the leftist line. But Bill Clinton never had the benefit of studying American government under George Carey while at Georgetown. Instead, as Clinton acknowledged in his acceptance speech at the 1992 Democratic convention, the professor who most shaped his views was Carroll Quigley, a committed liberal who taught history in the School of Foreign Service. I never took any courses from Dr. Quigley, but I understand that he had a great influence on the thinking of many of his students. Most of my activities as chairman of the College Republicans from 1965 to 1967 had to do with battling the New Left over Vietnam and related issues. By this time, many influential university institutions had fallen under the ideological control of the student radicals.

One of the most important organizations controlled by the Left was the National Student Association (NSA), an umbrella association of student governments on major college campuses across the country. It was extremely well-funded by major American foundations, including the Ford and Rockefeller foundations, and represented U.S. student opinion at major international youth conferences. The leadership of NSA was strongly opposed to American policy in Vietnam, branding the United States as the "aggressor." As a result of NSA's consistent leftist stances on major foreign and domestic policy issues, young conservatives led a fight to encourage colleges and universities to drop their affiliation with it. The efforts resulted in more than 150 colleges and universities tossing NSA off campus and almost as many voted to disaffiliate soon after they had joined.

As an opponent of NSA, I debated on many occasions the issue of whether its views were so extreme that student governments should withdraw from the organization. I couldn't understand how NSA was able to persuade prominent organizations to give them so much money. So, I took the opportunity to ask NSA president Phil Sherbourne directly about their finances. We flew down on the same plane from D.C. to a college in Virginia to debate the merits of membership in the NSA. He told me there was a "kindly" businessman in Boston who was very interested in encouraging student involvement in public affairs and that he was a big financial supporter of theirs. Phil was suitably vague when I pressed for more specifics. So I didn't pursue the point, although I didn't understand why some American businessman would give large chunks of money to a far left student organization. We went on with our debate, and I didn't give the matter much thought until shortly before I was to enter military service. The story broke in February 1967 that the "kindly" businessman the NSA president had referred to was apparently a CIA case officer. In addition to receiving funds from the Rockefeller and Ford foundations, NSA was getting substantial sums of money through CIA fronts. Altogether, CIA-provided tax dollars amounting to more than $3 million went into NSA's coffers.

It was quite a shock to me and to so many other young conservatives to discover that our own government through the CIA was providing left-wing student leaders with a significant percentage of their financial support. Here we were as the National College Republicans trying to make do on a budget in the tens of thousands of dollars while NSA was getting huge sums of money from the CIA. It was disillusioning to see the stupidity of the U.S. foreign policy makers at work in an arena with which I was intimately acquainted.

The CIA's rationalization for the funding of NSA was that it helped them get information on foreign student leaders and movements as a result of NSA's leaders attending international student conferences. While the CIA may have gleaned some information of minor value as a result of these overseas contacts, the damage done domestically was immeasurable. Our own government was funding a student organization that was working closely with New Left activists whose aim was to bring down the American political system.

The public disclosure of CIA funding must have been quite a traumatic experience for NSA's leaders. Here was a leftist student organization regularly denouncing, both at home and abroad, American foreign policy, only to have it revealed publicly that a majority of its annual budget came from the CIA covertly through the channels of various cooperative tax-exempt foundations. Apparently, NSA had become so dependent on CIA money by early 1967 that there was a vigorous debate among NSA board members (even after the public disclosure of the CIA connection) over whether to continue the CIA relationship in some other clandestine fashion. Finally, the NSA board decided to end its relationship with the agency. Its chairman, Sam Brown, issued the following statement:

> The National Supervisory Board of the National Student Association unanimously favors severing all ties with the [CIA]. The Board is currently considering the extent of NSA's relations with the CIA, ways to insure that all ties are eliminated, and internal reforms to insure it will not happen again.

New Left leader Sam Brown later would head up the Anti-Vietnam Moratorium Committee which held a massive protest against the war in 1968. One of his organizers for that demonstration was Bill Clinton. In 1977 Brown was appointed by President Jimmy Carter as director of ACTION, an independent federal agency in charge of volunteer programs such as VISTA and the Peace Corps.

As the sixties neared its conclusion, those of us who called ourselves conservatives appeared to be relegated to the losing side in American politics. Our political hero Barry Goldwater had gone down in flames in the 1964 presidential election, and now the New Left had surpassed the conservatives as the most influential political movement on America's campuses.

But, for the moment, my mind was focused on other matters. I was on my way to army basic training at Fort Bragg, North Carolina.

7

Ticket Punchers

Arguing theoretically that it made sense to stop Communist advances in Southeast Asia was, as I soon discovered, not quite the same as being an enlisted man in the army training for likely military service in Vietnam. I can't say that basic training was one of the more pleasant experiences in my life, but it did give me a good dose of badly needed humility. There is nothing like going from being a big fish in a small pond to crawling through the muddy clay at Fort Bragg on a wet and cold evening with machine guns firing overhead.

Our platoon was made up of a mixture of Southern whites and inner city blacks. Some of us had enlisted, others had been drafted. I was surprised to discover that I was the only college graduate in my platoon who was RA (regular army). Every other college-educated trainee was either ER (enlisted reserve) or NG (National Guard).

It began to dawn on me that most of the "citizen-soldiers" who were fighting this war were lower-middle and middle-class guys who joined the military, or were drafted, after they left high school or dropped out of college. There were other twenty-two- or twenty-three-year-old college grads in my platoon, but all of them were looking forward to only six months of active duty stateside in the Reserve or the Guard before returning home. Their chances of going to Vietnam were practically nil, while most of the rest of us were ticketed for service to Indochina.

I still remember a corporal who had served in Vietnam and was completing his military obligation at Fort Bragg asking me why I was such a stupid college grad. At first I didn't know what he was talking about; I must have had a quizzical look on my face. He went on to ask me why I was RA, instead of ER or NG. What was wrong with me that I couldn't figure out how to get out of going to Vietnam like all these other college guys? I laughed, although by then I have to admit I was beginning to wonder if perhaps I was a "damned fool" for having signed up for three years.

The young corporal's remark stuck with me over the years because it was obvious he had figured out how the rules of the draft favored those who knew how to "work" the system.

Once I was in the military, I quickly discovered that I didn't actually have all the answers on how to conduct the war in Vietnam. I was already skeptical about the civilian policy makers. I still believed that our military leaders knew what they were doing. I soon discovered that our Vietnam-era military had its own set of peculiar problems. Just like other major institutions in our society in the sixties, the American military was showing the effects of an increasingly bureaucratic and depersonalized society.

One of the first things that I noticed in basic training was that the military buildup in South Vietnam, had stretched our logistical and leadership resources almost to the limit.

As a recruit at Fort Bragg, I had assumed that the army would place a significant emphasis on making sure that those first eight weeks of initiation into military service were productive. When it came to the physical regimen demanded of us and the training in basic military skills, the army had a good system in place. It was a tough grind that taxed the individual both physically and mentally, but one that was absolutely critical in light of the fact that many of us would be sent to Vietnam within a few months. With half a million soldiers in country at that time, the rotation policy then in effect required a lot of warm bodies to replace soldiers who had completed their tour of duty or who had been killed or wounded in the war zone. Fort Bragg was doing its part to supply large numbers of young soldiers as replacements.

At the time, I didn't realize the kind of pressure the military command at Fort Bragg and other training units must have been under to turn an unusually large number of civilians into soldiers over an eight-week period. All that I could see from my limited vantage point as a basic trainee was that the quality of military leadership in the basic training camp where I had been assigned left a lot to be desired.

Our platoon sergeant loved to jump out of airplanes but was ill-equipped to mold raw recruits into good soldiers. One of our training instructors was a nineteen-year-old OCS (officer candidate school) lieutenant who relished being saluted by the enlisted men under his command. I particularly remember one class he taught on what our obligations were under the military code of conduct if we were ever captured by the enemy. After he finished reciting the textbook view as to what we were to do if we were taken prisoner, he proceeded to inform us that the Communists would never take *him* alive. I remember thinking that I wouldn't want to serve under his command in Vietnam. He would be the kind of lieutenant who would get his men into trouble.

Two years later in Vietnam, when I first got word of the My Lai incident where Vietnamese civilians were killed by a U.S. military unit commanded by Lieutenant William Calley, my first thoughts were of that young, cocky lieutenant at Fort Bragg. Most of us knew there were some ninety-day wonders (as the OCS officers were called at the time) who were too immature, too inexperienced, or too scared to be thrust into a combat leadership role. But the military needed the "bodies." Thus, we were bound to have our share of Lieutenant Calleys. It was just unfortunate for everyone concerned that Calley wound up being thrust into a situation he couldn't handle. As a result, a lot of people, including Calley himself, paid a very heavy price. But I suspect that is the case in all wars when a nation suddenly has to mobilize its young civilians faster than they can be trained. We needed large numbers of soldiers, and that included young lieutenants as well as infantry troopers. Most of the young officers grew up quickly in Vietnam and did their job well under very difficult circumstances, but a few went the way of Lieutenant Calley and got themselves and their men in trouble.

Some people in the military believed that you could put practically anyone in a command position if you gave him the proper training. As I was to observe throughout my tenure in the army, a military which had expanded enormously in terms of troop strength almost overnight found itself faced with an uneven caliber of leadership throughout its ranks.

I came to greatly admire many career military officers and enlisted men with whom I served or whom I got to know during my Vietnam service. Their pay was low, their hours were long and irregular, and they were always being uprooted from their current "home" and shipped to a new duty assignment. When career soldiers were assigned to Vietnam, not only did they have to leave their families behind, they also were stationed in a war zone where they were at risk of injury or death. Those military professionals who were there because of their commitment to mission and country had my utmost respect then, and will always have, because I saw up close what kind of sacrifices these men made to do their job. Yet, during the Vietnam era, a lot of those we called "ticket punchers" made their way up the ranks of the military command structure both stateside and in Vietnam.

For example, before embarking on my first assignment after arriving in Vietnam, I was ushered into the office of the commander of 525 MI for a personal briefing, along with some other new officers. The colonel didn't have much to say about the current intelligence situation in Vietnam. Nor did he focus on the overall intelligence responsibilities of our unit. Instead, he dwelt on how he was making the military intelligence branch more "military" in nature and how much easier it was these days, with the war going on in Vietnam, to make rank in Intelligence.

I suppose the colonel thought his speech would inspire us to consider a career in army intelligence, but it had the opposite effect on me. I thought that we were in Vietnam to defeat the Communists, not simply to speed promotions for military careerists. Moreover, given the nature of the kind of work I would be involved with as a case officer or agent handler, I had been told from my days in training at Fort Holabird that we should look and act like civilians since our undercover work generally required us to adopt a civilian "cover." Here, we had the head of 525 MI in Vietnam telling would-be intelligence operatives that we were going to out-soldier even the best infantrymen. The colonel's slogan was "Let's put the 'M' back into MI." (Some of those serving under the colonel joked that a more appropriate slogan would be "Let's take the 'I' out of MI.")

I later learned that the colonel had transferred out of the infantry because he couldn't make rank there, and into the intelligence branch because there were greater opportunities for promotion. How he managed to be put in charge of one of our most sensitive intelligence units in Vietnam is beyond my comprehension.

I attended a going away party in Can Tho for a young major who was being transferred to a six month assignment in a command position at the headquarters unit in Saigon. In his remarks that evening, the major told the assembled soldiers that, while he hated to leave, his new assignment in Saigon carried with it a command position, and, of course, command was what this war was all about for a career military officer.

I am sure that the career officer, who was a personable enough fellow, had no inkling of the effect his words had on people like me—noncareer soldiers who had either volunteered for, or been drafted into, military service. We could not have cared less about whether the war afforded career officers a greater opportunity for promotion. Officers more interested in "punching their career ticket" than in doing a good job and taking care of their men never won the respect of their own troops.

In his book *Soldier,* Lieutenant Colonel Anthony Herbert aptly describes the contrasting types of military leadership in Vietnam and the consequent performance of the young soldier:

> The average grunt or sergeant in Vietnam would do anything you told him to. They were almost fatalistic about it. As long as it was legitimate and you were out there with them, it was OK, no matter what the chances

of getting blown away. If you were out there with them, doing what they had to do, not trying to win promotions and decorations, then they'd do it all....There are people in the Army now who say that the troops that went over to Vietnam were a bunch of bums. But the people who are doing the crying are the people who are at fault. It was bad leadership that made some of these troops into substandard performers. Men just won't go out and fight and die for somebody who doesn't care about them, never sees them, never shares their risks while they're out doing the bleeding. If the troops didn't perform like the generals wanted them to, it was because the generals weren't doing their job. It's that simple.

In addition to the problems associated with the excessive emphasis on promotions, a bureaucratic decision was in force to give as many career officers as possible "command time" by rotating men in and out of these command assignments on a six month basis. This fostered a "getting your ticket punched" mentality among certain career officers. A policy of six month assignments may have made the personnel records of many servicemen look better, but it didn't do much for the overall war effort. The theory behind this policy was that command time in a hostile environment was important to the career development of a professional officer. From the standpoint of winning the war, however, achieving military success was made more difficult when a senior officer was transferred to another assignment just when he was "getting the hang of his job." In fact, the very idea of requiring soldiers to serve only a one year tour of duty in Vietnam did not make a lot of sense from a military standpoint (although I will be the first to admit that, from a personal perspective, that was just fine with me). When many of us finally had developed the knowledge and expertise to be effective intelligence officers in Vietnam, it was just about time to go home. That was not a good way to run a war.

8

Reporting on
the War

My own experience in the Delta had made me very skeptical about the news reporting on the war. This confirmed my initial impression formed in early 1966, while presenting the petition drive to Vice President Humphrey, that the mainstream press had turned against the war effort.

In *Roots of Radicalism,* two of the leading analysts of the American media's coverage of politics, Stanley Rothman and Robert Lichter, refer to the "media breakthrough" of the New Left which they assert took place in late 1965, right around the time of the College Republicans' national petition campaign. Being in the middle of the battle, I would concur with their assessment:

> Many liberal journalists either initially shared the sentiments of the antiwar demonstrators or had been converted by their arguments. But between the reformist sentiments of the antiwar protestors and the increasingly militant New Left elements, a widening gulf was

71

forming. The press coverage of the period seemed not to distinguish between the two. In this first period of "United front" antiwar activity, favorable articles on SDS and the movement appeared in radical journals like *The Nation,* liberal magazines like *The New Republic,* and even major mainstream media outlets like the *New York Times* and *Newsweek.* At the same time, Movement celebrities began to appear on national television programs. This development culminated in controversial appearances by radicals like (Tom) Hayden and (Stokeley) Carmichael on "The Dick Cavett Show."

Often, what American journalists were writing seemed to reflect little more than a superficial analysis of the conflict. From what I read, it appeared that a lot of reporters had preconceived opinions which shaped their coverage. For a few reporters, our side could do no wrong; according to their stories, we clearly were winning the war. More typically, however, journalists were vehement opponents of the war; their coverage reflected their hostility toward American policy in Vietnam.

One of the few exceptions to what had become by then my general rule that most American reporters in Vietnam wrote stories to conform to their ideological biases was Peter Kann of the *Wall Street Journal.* Kann was a hardworking journalist who did his best to report objectively on a war laden with ambiguities. He was particularly knowledgeable about the Viet Cong infrastructure and the political side of the war.

Kann came to Chau Doc while I was there to look into reports that hundreds of Cambodians, who supposedly had been operating their own private army in Cambodia, had turned themselves in to the Americans. In addition to turning in their weapons, they were seeking status as "chieu hois." At the time there was a major effort underway to encourage "chieu hois," who were Viet Cong guerrillas and other military opponents of the government, to come over to our side without fear of retribution. In fact, there were substantial rewards handed out to "chieu hois" for defecting. Admiral Zumwalt, then the American commander of our naval forces in Vietnam and a man who understood the value of public relations, tried to turn this into a major PR victory for our side. Zumwalt had become well known for sending out what he called "Z grams" as a method of garnering press attention, and he alerted the media to this success story unfolding in Chau Doc.

There was only a slight problem with the story. These weren't legitimate chieu hois. I had talked to a few of the men through a Cambodian interpreter, and their stories conflicted as to where they had been based and what battle action they had seen. Most of the weapons they brought in with them were vintage World War II, of little or no use to anyone but collectors. With the assistance of my Vietnamese interpreter who uncovered some additional information, I finally pieced together most of the story and quickly contacted the Cambodian desk officer of Strategic Research & Analysis (SRA) in Saigon to tell him that these Cambodians weren't "chieu hois" who had defected from Cambodia but were Cambodians who lived in Vietnam and were trying to use this ruse to avoid the draft while picking up a little extra money for themselves.

Peter Kann was the only reporter who bothered to come to the scene of the story and check it out for himself. He figured out quickly what the truth was and was on his way. I imagine that the PR guys working for Zumwalt did some fancy footwork in order to make the Chau Doc "chieu hois" story, which they had promoted so heavily, fade away.

While I was stationed at SRA, the My Lai incident surfaced in a story by Seymour Hersch, who had been reporting on the war for the Dispatch News Service—an independent, leftist news organ.

A young OCS lieutenant named William Calley had overseen and participated in a massacre of innocent women and children in a small Vietnamese village known as My Lai. The mainstream media suddenly had the type of story that could truly embarrass the American war effort, and maximum publicity was given this tragic incident.

If all you learned about our young infantry officers in Vietnam was what the major media told you in the wake of the My Lai massacre, you wouldn't have a very high opinion of our young soldiers. But for every Lieutenant Calley, there were dozens of men like Captain Pete Scott who molded a group of Vietnamese and ethnic Cambodians into an effective fighting force in a Viet Cong-infested area of the Delta known as Nui Co To, or the Seven Mountains.

Pete was loyal to the people who worked for him and respectful of the Vietnamese culture, and his men responded in kind. Captain Scott was a good officer and a fine human being, but you never read any stories about young officers like him in the *New York Times*. His wasn't a story mainstream journalists wanted to report. The only national magazine that I remember at the time that had anything good to say about our soldiers in Vietnam was the *Reader's Digest*. There was a particularly fine article on how American soldiers were trying to help Vietnamese kids in need, written by a young journalist named Ken Tomlinson (now editor in chief of the *Digest*), who had been one of our college Republican leaders from Virginia back in the Goldwater days.

Most Americans who got their news from the mainstream media publications like *Time, Newsweek,* and the national television networks saw the Calley incident portrayed not as an aberration of American behavior in Vietnam, but as an example of how our young soldiers were treating the Vietnamese people. This false depiction of the "typical" American soldier as a murderer of innocent women and children not only had a negative impact at home in terms of public support for our soldiers, it also helped fuel an animosity toward our soldiers that led some opponents of the war to greet returning veterans by hurling epithets at them such as "Welcome home, baby killer."

In 1970, after returning from Vietnam, I was involved with the White House Fellowship program (more on this later). Time-Life hosted a reception and dinner for us in New York. Our host for the evening was Richard Clurman who was then publisher of the magazine group. Clurman had invited some prominent figures from the media including Mike Wallace of CBS, Sander Vanocur of NBC, and Warren Phillips, publisher of the *Wall Street Journal*. The evening was billed as an off-the-record exchange of views on government between the White House Fellows and leaders of the media.

At the reception, the waiters not only poured strong drinks but were quick to provide refills. I became concerned that some of the

White House Fellows might be a little too "open" in their comments as the evening wore on. Since the Fellows were special assistants to cabinet officers and high level White House officials, they had access to a lot of sensitive information. With people having a few drinks in them and put in a friendly mood to have a frank exchange of views with the media, one of our group might say something inadvertently that could hurt the administration and create problems for the Fellowship program itself.

After dinner, we retired to the board room where place cards had been set up for the approximately forty people. Each of us with the Fellowship program was seated next to a representative of the media. Richard Clurman of *Time* started the "dialogue" by launching into a discussion of the Nixon administration. In light of my concern that something said "off the record" by one of our people might create some problems for the program, I got the "bright idea" of changing the topic of discussion from the Nixon administration to the media's coverage of the war in Vietnam. That was easy enough to arrange since it was such an appropriate topic of conversation in light of the makeup of the assembled group. So instead of discussing the inner workings of the Nixon administration, we spent the rest of the evening listening to some leading members of the journalistic establishment give us their views on media responsibility in reporting on the war.

By that time, our media hosts were also "well-lubricated." As a result, they were much more frank in voicing their real sentiments on the war than they might have been otherwise.

One nationally-known network personality, Sander Vanocur, lamented that he had once said something positive about American efforts to oppose Communism in Vietnam. He then proceeded to denounce everything associated with our war effort. As we listened to him rant on and on about all the terrible things we were doing in Vietnam, the NBC newsman made it clear that he thought we were the "bad guys" in the war. The opinions he voiced that evening didn't sound all that different from those I had heard expressed many times by various leftist critics of the war I had debated over the years. It was a shock to me, however, to hear a well-respected national media figure spew forth a grab bag of simplistic, leftist cliches about the war. The vehemence of his denunciation of our policy was in vivid contrast to the public image he had fostered as an objective journalist. Most of the other members of the media present that evening voiced similar opposition to Nixon's war policy, although perhaps not with the passion displayed by Vanocur.

Warren Phillips at least made the case that the press had an obligation to maintain objectivity in reporting on the war. And, to his credit, CBS's Mike Wallace praised General Creighton Abrams' leadership of our troops in Vietnam. However, the only journalist present who actually defended the American effort to defeat Communism in South Vietnam was Dan Seligman, a young reporter with *Fortune* magazine.

It was already obvious to those of us who closely followed the coverage of the war that the mainstream media had turned against American policy in Vietnam. What I didn't realize until that evening was how intense their opposition had become and how closely aligned their views were to those on the Left who blamed America for the war.

Robert Elegant later spelled all this out in an article in *Encounter.* In "How the Media Lost the War," he revealed how prominent American journalists had let their opposition to the war influence their reporting on what was happening in Vietnam. In that piece Elegant, who covered the war for the *Los Angeles Times,* made the case for the proposition that media bias played a significant part in our ultimate defeat in Indochina.

9

Ensuring Defeat

By the end of my tour of duty in Vietnam, I was filled with conflicting feelings about the war, our military leaders, and the civilian policy makers who had gotten us into this war of "gradualism."

As for our military leadership in Vietnam, my year there had exposed me to a mixed bag of career military officers. But I still have fond recollections of outstanding leaders like Colonel Lee who represented for me the professional military at its best.

I had the same feeling about the late General Creighton Abrams, who was the commander of American military forces during the year I was in Vietnam. Although I never personally worked for him, our office briefed General Abrams on a study I had done on the political strategy of the North Vietnamese revolutionary theorist, Truong Chinh. As the briefing officer told me afterwards, the General displayed a depth of knowledge about our North Vietnamese foes which was unusual for senior American officers. Too often, it had seemed to me, we Americans hadn't paid enough attention to the objectives of our enemy and how they planned to achieve them. The more I saw General Abrams in action, the more I thought that we had a military leader in charge of our forces who knew what needed to be done to win the war if the civilian policy makers would only listen to him.

When it came to our civilian policy makers, those who had made such a mess of the Vietnam war, I viewed Robert McNamara as the principal architect of our defeat. Secretary of defense under Presidents Kennedy and Johnson (followed by Clark Clifford), McNamara instituted the strategy of "gradualism" which sought to contain but not defeat North Vietnamese aggression. To gradualism, he linked his faulty theories of "quantifiable analysis." Its purpose was to try to statistically measure the success or failure of our military effort. In so doing, I believe, he blindly and stubbornly assured failure.

The McNamara attempt to measure success in quantitative terms filtered down to every level of the governmental bureaucracy, afflicting the military command structure as well as civilian policy makers. The most notorious example of this mind-set at work was the "body count" game in which our soldiers were told to go to extraordinary lengths to report enemy KIA (killed in action) and WIA (wounded in action).

You could see the footprints of the McNamara approach everywhere as our officials emphasized the importance of quantifiable data in measuring the success of the war—this at the expense of sound military judgment and a winning strategy.

To judge the relative security of the Vietnamese population in the hamlets from the threat of the Viet Cong, the McNamara crowd had developed something called the Hamlet Evaluation System (HES) which was designed to give officials a statistical read-out on how well we were doing. On a regular basis, American and Vietnamese officials in charge of each province would be required to file a report on the relative security of the populace in each hamlet, village, and district within the province. A little common sense and understanding of human nature should have made our policy makers aware of the severe limitations of such a quantitative approach to measuring overall security.

If I were a Vietnamese province chief or the senior American province adviser, how would it look on my record if the province

I was responsible for showed up on the HES report as less secure vis-á-vis the Viet Cong than the security statistics under my predecessor? Add to the equation the possibility that my predecessor already had inflated the security figures to make himself look better. If I inherit a province that, according to HES, is 92 percent secure from the Viet Cong, do I send to headquarters a statistical breakdown that indicates my province is less secure from the Communists than when I took it over? Or do I perpetuate the fraud that was started before I arrived and show a statistical improvement in my HES report?

The temptation to take the latter course was obvious to any of us on the scene, particularly with the heavy application of continuing pressure from above to show tangible signs of improvement.

In what should have been anticipated, this charade of claiming steady improvement in security against potential Communist attacks throughout South Vietnam through the HES statistical measurements blew up in our face with the Communist Tet offensive in February, 1968.

Even though American troops and our South Vietnamese allies ultimately dealt the Viet Cong a major defeat at that time, our faulty statistical evaluation system on security in the South provided a lot of ammunition for critics of the war who argued that our government couldn't be trusted to tell the American people the truth about the real situation.

The failure of HES undermined the credibility of any of our officials who tried to make the case that the Tet offensive turned out to be a major military setback for the Viet Cong and their North Vietnamese sponsors. The irony is that in that one instance the officials were right—Tet was a big victory for our side as Peter Braestrup so cogently explained in his analysis of Tet entitled *The Big Story.*

A military victory for us was turned into a propaganda defeat, and part of the reason was that we had overpromised on the security issue with a flawed measurement system that was typical of the McNamara approach to warfare.

This penchant for statistical measurement also extended itself to military intelligence units like 525 MI which fell into the trap of measuring results by the quantity of intelligence reports. It paid a price for such a delusion by generating a lot of so-called intelligence information that had little real value.

Another of McNamara's brilliant ideas to win the war through technology was the development of an electronic device that looked like a small buffalo chip. It was supposed to be dropped along the South Vietnam border with Cambodia, Laos, and North Vietnam. Its purpose was to detect Communist infiltration of troops into South Vietnam. As I learned for myself when I was in Chau Doc along the Cambodian border where the device was utilized, there was only one small problem—water buffalo and other animals crossing the border also set off the device.

Finally, there was the problem of Americans trying to do much of the job of defeating the Communists rather than merely assisting South Vietnam in *its* fight to remain free. I suspect that our most fatal mistake in this regard had occurred back in 1963 when we encouraged, and collaborated in, the overthrow of President Diem. Thereafter, it became an American war. As one South Vietnamese colonel put it, "American aid is like opium. Our people have become dependent upon it, and we have let the Americans do what we ought to be doing for ourselves." When the opium (in the form of American military assistance) was withdrawn, the South Vietnamese were not strong enough to withstand the Communist onslaught.

The Vietnam war was a devastating experience for us as a nation. Yet had American policy been different, had we adopted a winning strategy and provided our men with the means and authority to defeat North Vietnam, and had we not fallen captive to the McNamara policy of gradualism which got us bogged down in the kind of war our enemy preferred to fight, then most of the problems associated with our South Vietnamese allies and our military performance would have faded into the background and ultimately been inconsequential in the larger scheme of things.

Ronald Reagan was right when he attacked our "no-win" strategy in Vietnam. We fought for a tie and wound up with a defeat.

10

Coming Home

After returning from Vietnam at the end of December, 1969, I was shocked to see so many people roughly my own age clearly "on the other side." Since I was in civilian clothes by then, nobody said anything to me about the military or Vietnam. Some of my fellow veterans were not so fortunate. In his book *Homecoming,* columnist Bob Greene recounts first person stories of returning veterans being subjected to various displays of abuse by antiwar activists. One veteran described being spat upon by a person "wearing a shirt that said 'Welcome Home Baby Killer.'" Many of my friends have recounted similar incidents that happened to them once back from Vietnam.

Before we went overseas, the American military had drummed into our heads the fact that a "cultural shock" awaited us when we got to Vietnam. With this forewarning, we were reasonably prepared for the dramatic cultural differences that we were exposed to once "in country." Almost to a man, however, Vietnam veterans were not prepared for the "reverse cultural shock" we would experience on our return to the United States. One young combat veteran described his return home in this way:

> Initially, I was exhilarated at being back home again. Getting out of Vietnam and the military in one live piece was like a cross between graduation and salvation. But the immediate excitement quickly wore off. Any mention of my being in combat in Vietnam brought reactions varying from coolness to hostility. I soon became restless at dealing with things that seemed to me mundane, unimportant, and boring. I put more of myself into my tour in Vietnam than any other experience in my life, living in violent extremes—days of combat and days of idleness. It was a matter of life and death. Yet at home people didn't understand or care, and treated me as though none of that made any difference.

Somehow along the way, much of the blame for what had gone wrong in Vietnam was laid on the shoulders of the Vietnam veteran. For those who cast the blame, it didn't seem to matter that the young American soldier in Vietnam wasn't responsible for the policy decisions about how (or whether) to fight that war. To the antiwar activists on the left, those of us who accepted our military obligation and went to Vietnam became identified with their enemy—an "imperialistic" American government bent on propping up a "corrupt" South Vietnamese "dictatorship." In its efforts to bring down the "enemy," the Left felt entitled to use every weapon in its propaganda arsenal. If that meant engaging in personal attacks on our young soldiers in Vietnam, well, so be it.

My first exposure to this phenomenon of "blaming the warrior for the war" occurred in 1965 when I observed the major protest against the war in Washington, D.C., organized by the Students for a Democratic Society. Not only were the youthful demonstrators at the rally carrying Viet Cong flags, they also were waving placards referring to our soldiers as "murderers" and "baby killers" while chanting ad nauseam the slogan "How many kids did you kill today?"

This depiction of our soldiers set the tone for a new mythology that American soldiers were unfeeling and uncaring murderers of innocent women and children in Vietnam—paid mercenaries, helping to prevent a popular revolutionary movement from coming to power in South Vietnam.

Throughout the war, leftist activists kept up a steady drumbeat of personalized attacks on our soldiers. The traditional image of the American soldier as hero had been twisted by the Left's potent propaganda machine into a new, negative stereotype. The young veteran saw himself referred to on television, in print, and in conversation as a drug addict and/or a psychologically disturbed killer. Often, members of his own peer group let him know in a variety of subtle, and not so subtle, ways that he had been a fool for winding up in Vietnam—for there were so many easy ways for a "smart" guy to avoid going. This constant denigration of the service of the American soldier in Vietnam took its toll on the returning veteran, who was initially bewildered at the hostility directed toward him by young people his own age.

The Left's efforts to portray the American soldier in Vietnam in the worst possible light were given a major boost when the story of the My Lai massacre broke in 1969. From the New Left's point of view, the charge that Lieutenant William Calley had ordered or condoned the murder of innocent Vietnamese civilians was akin to hitting the mother lode. This gave radical leaders like Tom Hayden the ammunition they needed. As he says in *Reunion:* "The scene of women, children, and babies mutilated and dumped in a long ditch would become the Guernica for my generation. 'I sent them a good boy, and they made him a murderer,' cried the mother of one of the soldiers at My Lai."

In previous wars, the returning soldiers were welcomed home as heroes. Not this time. Our generation was so deeply split over Vietnam that the veteran paid the price with a homecoming that typically ranged from indifference to open hostility. Most of us were confused enough by all the changes that had occurred back home while we were gone. Now, we had to deal also with this image of ourselves as "murderers" and "baby killers."

After a few weeks in Dallas visiting family and friends, it was time for me to return to work. I landed a temporary job in Washington as a consultant with the White House Conference on Children and Youth. This was one of those congressionally mandated sessions which took place once a decade. The ostensible purpose of the gathering was to bring together delegates from around the country to discuss governmental policies affecting children and youth.

This particular conference was turning into a potential "can of worms" for the Nixon administration. Anything having to do with youth in 1970 inevitably got bogged down in the controversy over Vietnam, and this proved no exception. Youthful opponents of the war wanted to turn it into a denunciation of Nixon's war policies while the administration wanted to keep the focus of the meeting on domestic issues. One problem for the president in this regard was that almost all of the young people on the White House conference staff were strongly opposed to our involvement in Vietnam. Many of them even sided with the New Left view that we were supporting the wrong side in the war.

I definitely felt out of place. The only other returning veteran on the staff was Ted Lunger, a former Special Forces captain who had worked with the Montagnards in Vietnam. The Montagnards were non-Vietnamese tribesmen who lived in the highlands region of Vietnam. American Special Forces teams had befriended them in the early sixties. And, ever since then, they had worked directly for the Green Berets. They were known for their opposition to the Viet Cong and their loyalty to their American friends.

Ted had led his band of irregulars in battles against the Viet Cong for control of certain sectors of the Delta, including the Seven Mountains region in Chau Doc province—my old stomping grounds. Both of us had strong feelings about the way the war was being fought. We also held conservative views which put us at odds with most of the other young people on the staff. We became fast friends.

But neither one of us stayed very long at the White House Conference on Children and Youth offices. As far as Ted and I were concerned, the top staffers there seemed more interested in "accommodating the Left" than in standing up to their demands. Since our views were "out of the mainstream," we ended our involvement with the Conference by mutual agreement.

I finally began to understand why so many of the young soldiers I had met during my trip to Vietnam as a civilian in 1966 had seemed distant. About the only people I felt comfortable with in talking about Vietnam after my return were people like me who had served there. With everybody else, I tended to avoid the subject of the war as much as possible. In part, this may have been because my own feelings about Vietnam were confused, particularly during my first year back.

Hoping for a victory in the war, I feared we were losing. Although I was impressed with the military leadership being provided by General Creighton Abrams, I had no confidence that the Washington policy makers would pursue effectively a strategy for winning the war. It seemed as though we were muddling through, doing just enough to prevent a defeat so that somehow we could negotiate ourselves out of this mess.

I was extended a number of invitations to speak to student audiences. Although I received a friendly reception from young people interested in hearing about Vietnam from someone who had been there, I quit speaking on the subject after only a couple of speeches. My views on the war were filled with "greys". It didn't make much sense for me to communicate my feelings to others until I had resolved some of the internal conflicts in my own mind about what we should do in Vietnam.

Yet, while in many ways I was unclear as to the best solution to our Vietnam quagmire, I had formed strong opinions about certain aspects of the war. For example, I favored President Nixon's policy of "Vietnamization" designed to reduce the American presence in Vietnam and turn over more of the running of the war to the South Vietnamese themselves.

I also deeply resented the fact that North Vietnamese and Viet Cong forces could use their sanctuaries in Cambodia and Laos as base camps and supply lines while these areas were supposedly off limits to our side. Hey, if we are in a war, aren't we there to win? Why should we give the enemy the advantage of safe havens in areas within the war zone? It didn't make any sense to me, particularly when I had seen numerous intelligence reports in 1969 pointing to a buildup of North Vietnamese forces in Cambodia as a prelude to what we believed would be a major attack sometime in 1970 against our forces in III and IV Corps. Having been based in Chau Doc on the Cambodian border during much of my tour, I thought that it was ludicrous that Communist forces could shell us with artillery from across the border, and we weren't supposed to respond. Or that their troops could attack and then scamper to safety into Communist-controlled areas of Cambodia.

I had been back in Washington for only a short while when Richard Nixon authorized a military operation in Cambodia designed to disrupt Communist sanctuaries there. It was a pre-emptive strike. We hit the enemy in a surprise attack before it had the opportunity to launch its own attack against our forces in the South. I was pleased that Nixon had exhibited the political courage to challenge this illusion that the war ended at the Cambodian border. I was convinced then, and remain convinced, that the Cambodian incursion saved many American and South Vietnamese lives that would have been needlessly lost had we waited for the North Vietnamese to attack us first from their Cambodian sanctuaries. From the reaction in Washington, D.C., however, one would have thought that the world was coming to an end. Anti-Vietnam protesters rushed to Washington to voice their opposition to Nixon's actions. Classes were shut down, and exams were canceled to accommodate the tens of thousands of draft-exempt students who descended on our nation's capital.

I went over to the steps of the Capitol and listened as Senator Charles Percy addressed a throng of assembled students. I became disgusted with what he had to say and how he said it. His speech was loaded with "weasel" words in an attempt to placate the students while not fully embracing their views. The Illinois Republican senator was your typical, middle-of-the-road politician trying to please both sides on the most controversial issue facing our nation at that time. Despite his best efforts, Percy wasn't able to satisfy the demonstrators or me; he definitely lost my respect.

From the Capitol steps, I went to the office of Congressman George Bush who had asked me to meet with a group of student demonstrators from Princeton University. I listened as the young people tried to convince Bush that the Cambodian operation was "immoral." Their arguments were loaded with cliches, but that was to be expected given the overwhelming mood of opposition to the war on the campuses by 1970. It was hard for me to get mad at these kids. They seemed so sincere, but they didn't know very much about what was going on in Vietnam. They just were against what Nixon was doing. They hadn't even considered whether or not this Cambodian operation might benefit our overall war effort and save the lives of American soldiers which otherwise might have been jeopardized in a major Communist attack.

I tried to explain some of these factors to them. While the discussion was polite enough, it was as though we were talking past each other. The respective prisms through which we analyzed the war were so radically different that there was very little common ground between me and the Princeton students.

My real quarrel, however, was with those within the anti-Vietnam movement who claimed that the Viet Cong represented the "progressive forces" in South Vietnam. I had seen enough evidence of Communist atrocities to know that a Marxist-Leninist regime in South Vietnam wasn't the solution to that nation's problems. Two decades later, we now understand the fatal flaws of this dying totalitarian ideology. But, at the time, the New Left was effective in portraying the Viet Cong as a progressive movement that would usher in a popular, socialist government to replace the Thieu-Ky "dictatorship."

Equally upsetting to me and other veterans I knew was the decision of some of our own to join the ranks of the opposition. With backing from the Left, an organization was formed calling itself the Vietnam Veterans Against the War (VVAW). A number of former military intelligence types became active in VVAW, including Jeff Stein, with whom I had gone through intelligence school at Fort Holabird. The guy whose conduct upset me the most was John Kerry of Massachusetts, a graduate of Yale University who had been a junior naval officer in Vietnam. Kerry would make regular appearances on the "Tonight" show, all decked out in his military fatigues, where he would proceed to denounce the American effort to defeat Communism in South Vietnam. He also made numerous appearances in Washington, becoming a regular (I am told) on the Georgetown cocktail party circuit. As far as I was concerned, Kerry was purely and simply an opportunist, parlaying his involvement in the antiwar movement into a budding political career. John Kerry is now a U.S. senator from Massachusetts.

It was frustrating to watch a guy like Kerry being anointed by the media as the spokesman for Vietnam veterans. While VVAW never managed to enlist the support of more than a small fraction of men who served in Vietnam, you never would have known that from the media's treatment of the organization. The guys who acknowledged their "guilt" for having served in Vietnam and "begged forgiveness" from the Left were held in high esteem by the mainstream press. At the time, I thought that something should be done to correct the false impression that spokesmen like Kerry represented the viewpoint of most of us. But there wasn't much support then for such an initiative.

It would take another decade before Vietnam veterans would finally band together to correct the record.

But more about that later.

11

A Temporary Stint
with the Credentialed
Society

Upon my return from Vietnam, I had not expected to go to work for the Nixon administration. Barry Goldwater was still my political hero. The uninspired brand of Republican politics that Richard Nixon represented didn't have much appeal to me. My only personal meeting with Nixon had taken place back in 1966 when I was national chairman of the College Republicans. I happened to be one of the speakers at a North Carolina Young Republican convention where the former vice president was the keynote speaker.

Before he spoke, I had the opportunity to visit privately with him. Nixon was a difficult man to warm up to. While he was obviously intelligent and knowledgeable, I sensed an impersonal quality about him that led me to conclude that having a conversation with a young Republican like myself was a duty he felt obligated to perform, but one that he surely didn't enjoy. I couldn't shake the negative impression of him that I had formed back in 1960 while watching the first televised presidential debate between him and John Kennedy. The former vice president gave a good talk that evening in 1966, focusing on American foreign policy, his area of primary interest, but I didn't come away from the convention ready to jump aboard the Nixon bandwagon.

Four years later, Richard Nixon was in the White House, and I was back in Washington having second thoughts about a Republican leader I had dismissed as too opportunistic for my taste. I was impressed with his Vietnam policy, however. Through his "Vietnamization" of the war, he was turning over more of the actual prosecution of the war to our South Vietnamese allies in an attempt to wean them away from an excessive reliance on American aid. Moreover, his willingness to take the war to the enemy by attacking Communist sanctuaries in Cambodia showed his intent to try to win the war, rather than simply play for a tie. Maybe I had been wrong about Nixon. One way to find out was to join his administration.

Having worked actively for the Republican party, I had gotten to know many of its leaders. As a result, I had the good fortune to have a number of friends in the administration willing to recommend me for a variety of posts. After leaving the temporary position at the White House Conference on Children and Youth, I sought a full-time job elsewhere in the administration. As it happened, I had the good fortune to be able to choose from among attractive opportunities at the United States Information Agency, the Small Business Administration, the Domestic Policy office at the White House, and the White House Fellowship program.

David Miller, whom I had known since my days as College Republican chairman, made me a proposal that was difficult to refuse. At the time he was the director of the White House Fellows, and he asked me to become the deputy director of the program. In addition to helping David run the office, I would be able to spend much of my time in an assignment similar to that given the Fellows, as a White House staff aide.

Miller had worked with John Dean, the new White House legal counsel, when both of them were at the Justice Department under John Mitchell. David also had a good, working relationship with Bud Krogh, who was John Ehrlichman's principal deputy. He provided me with the appropriate introductions to Dean and Krogh, and both of them offered me the opportunity to work for them as a policy analyst. So, I accepted Miller's offer and also went to work for the White House counsel's office on a part-time basis.

My only reservation about accepting the position as Miller's deputy was that our political views were so dissimilar. While I was an outspoken conservative, David was a liberal Republican from the Nelson Rockefeller-John Lindsay wing of the party. A graduate of Harvard University and a former White House Fellow, he was much more in tune than I with the belief system of the "liberal elites" who set the policy agenda in Washington.

This thirtyish, young "corporate liberal" also was committed to finding a way to bridge the political gap between the Left and the Right. To me that was a futile exercise, particularly in light of the fundamental differences between conservatives and New Leftists over such controversial issues as Vietnam. We have an expression down in Texas which fits Miller's attempt to resolve that sixties, intragenerational dispute: "He who stands in the middle of the road gets run over." I don't think he understood how deeply divided the two sides were.

Nonetheless, I liked David personally and figured that we would be able to work together at the Fellowship program in spite of our differences.

The Fellowship post, combined with my work for the White House counsel, provided me with an interesting vantage point from which to observe the inner workings of the Nixon administration. It also enabled me to gain an insight into the mind-set of the liberal elites who, as I soon discovered, exercised a significant influence over the White House Fellowship program even during a Republican administration.

The White House Fellowship program was originated by John Gardner, a quintessential Establishment figure, who was the secretary of the Department of Health, Education, and Welfare (HEW) under President Lyndon Johnson. The program sought to recruit outstanding young men and women, between the ages of twenty-three and thirty-five, who would spend one year at the highest levels of the federal government as special assistants to cabinet officers or as White House aides.

During the year I was with the program, over a thousand candidates applied for the fifteen to twenty available Fellowships.

Sixteen men and one woman, Julia Vadela, were named White House Fellows for the 1970-71 period. The average age of the Fellows was thirty, and five members of the group were military officers. Reading the resumés of the Fellows, I was very impressed with the background and achievements of almost all of them. Winning a White House Fellowship was comparable to being selected a Rhodes Scholar as Bill Clinton had been in 1968. Many of the Fellows took advantage of that experience in Washington, and that credential added to their resumé, to achieve later prominence in business, the military, and/or government service.

For example, Robert (Bud) McFarlane was a marine lieutenant colonel when he won a White House Fellowship in 1971. He later worked as a foreign policy aide to Henry Kissinger and Senator John Tower. After his retirement from the military, he joined the Reagan administration in 1981 as State Department counselor. Bud later was named by the president as his national security adviser. Unfortunately, he became embroiled in the Iran-Contra affair and was forced to resign. Nonetheless, were it not for his initial selection as a White House Fellow in 1971, I believe that it is fair to say that Bud McFarlane never would have risen to such a position of influence over American foreign policy. That opportunity to work on the Nixon White House staff from 1971 to 1972 proved to be an enormous boost to his career prospects.

As Deputy Director, I was responsible for setting up the education program. Working in conjunction with David Miller, I arranged for the Fellows to meet in off-the-record discussions with prominent members of the Nixon administration, leaders of Congress, and well-known figures from the private sector. Our guests that year included George Romney, Clark Clifford, John Kenneth Galbraith, the Rockefellers (David, John D. III, Jay, and Nelson), David Broder, Garry Wills, John Sears, Larry O'Brien, Admiral Thomas Moorer, Melvin Laird, Richard Clurman, Mike Wallace, and many others. In addition, we visited with foreign leaders on trips to Latin America, the Soviet Union, and Eastern Europe.

To me, these discussions were the most stimulating part of the Fellowship program. The opportunity to engage in candid conversations with some of the most prominent leaders in government, big business, and the media obviously was informative. But it was more than that. These discussions allowed us to have an inside "peek" into the mind-set of what would be called (for the lack of a better term) the American Establishment. Listening to the views of people like David Rockefeller, Richard Clurman, et al., we could come to an informed opinion as to whether or not their prescriptions for making America a better country made sense.

The encounter at the reception given by Time-Life, described earlier, was one such example. Another such meeting was with attorney Clark Clifford, a premier Washington insider and the secretary of defense under Lyndon Johnson. The subject of Vietnam came up. Clifford was discussing the leadership split in Communist North Vietnam. He described it to us in terms of "hawks vs. doves." The more he talked, the more apparent it became how little he really knew about the complex leadership dispute that was taking place in North Vietnam. Clifford suggested to the Fellows that one faction of Communist leaders in the North wanted peace on reasonable terms while the other faction (made up of Communist "hawks") was intent on prosecuting the war. As I knew from my access to top secret documents on the political situation in North Vietnam, the reality of the leadership struggle there was quite different from what Clifford was describing. Both factions in the North were determined to persist in the struggle to take over South Vietnam. The dispute was over strategy. Additionally, one faction led by Truong Chinh was more closely aligned to the Chinese Communists while the other group was pro-Soviet.

One might expect to read such a simplistic analysis as this "hawk vs. dove" thesis from some wet-behind-the-ears, young reporter for *Newsweek* magazine. However, it was a shock to hear such nonsense being uttered by a man reputed to be one of the smartest Washington lawyers, one who had replaced Robert McNamara in overseeing the conduct of the war for Lyndon Johnson.

It was as though "the emperor had no clothes." This highly respected liberal insider knew a hell of a lot less about what was going on in Vietnam than many young Americans, half his age or less, who had served there. It was further evidence that the "reputations" and "resumés" of prominent Establishment leaders often covered their lack of real knowledge and insight into perplexing problems like Vietnam.

All too often, so-called public policy experts whom we met with that year as part of the Fellowship educational program were more opinionated and less knowledgeable than I had expected. It seemed to me that too many of these Establishment insiders tried to force the objective data to conform with their particular worldview when an honest searcher of the truth would have come to different conclusions based on the evidence.

Ever since my year in Washington with the Fellowship program, I have been more than a little skeptical about relying on "experts."

Although I didn't know it at the time I was asked by David Miller to serve as his deputy director, the Fellowship program was under attack from conservatives within the Nixon administration for being too liberal, too elitist, and too skewed toward the ideology of the national Democratic party. Pat Buchanan, then a speechwriter for Richard Nixon, was leading the charge to reform the Fellowship program or get rid of it. I later concluded that Miller had offered me the job to get right-wingers like Buchanan off his back, since I was known to be a conservative Republican.

It didn't take me long to figure out why conservatives within the administration weren't happy with the operation. Even in a Republican administration, the regional panels which chose the national finalists were loaded with Establishment liberals and Ivy League graduates who tended to favor candidates who had a degree from Harvard or Yale and held "politically correct" views on Vietnam and other major issues. I sat in on a number of these regional meetings and had the opportunity to observe and participate in the grilling of the candidates.

The most memorable session was in Boston. The panel's chairman was retired Major General James A. Gavin, famous for his now-discredited "enclave theory" for fighting in Vietnam. Essentially, Gavin proposed that the United States withdraw its forces into enclaves and adopt a defensive approach to stopping the Communist attempt to overrun South Vietnam. Most knowledgeable experts on the war dismissed the Gavin concept as a screwy idea, but he was a liberal "hero" at the time because he was viewed as a "military dove" on the war. And there weren't many of those with the rank of general. Besides, he had been an accomplished military commander during World War II. So his views had been widely, and favorably, publicized in the media.

However, I quickly discerned that day that the real power among the panelists was Edwin Canham, the editor of the *Christian Science Monitor* and a leading Eastern liberal. Canham also chaired the Rhodes Scholars panel for the Boston region.

One candidate who came before the panel was head and shoulders above all others in qualifications, experience, and ability. He was a graduate of the Naval Academy and an active duty lieutenant commander who had served with distinction in Vietnam. At the time, he was pursuing a graduate degree in international relations at the Fletcher School of Diplomacy where he was first in his class. In person he made a good appearance and presented his views in a thoughtful and articulate manner. A sure winner, I thought, and a man who would be a real asset to the Nixon administration. But as panelists Gavin and Canham questioned the naval officer, it soon became clear that his views were an obstacle to his selection. He did not endorse Gavin's "enclave theory" and had the audacity to assert that we should, and could, win the war in Vietnam.

After a few comments in this vein, it was obvious to me that the candidate didn't stand a chance of being selected as a finalist. As I could observe from the expressions on their faces and the tone of their questions, Canham and Gavin were not about to let this naval officer be selected as a White House Fellow. Not only were his views unacceptable, it was clear that his convictions were deeply held and that he would not be easily dissuaded from them. This was not the kind of young leader that liberals took a shine to. He was not the malleable type and unknowingly paid a personal price that day for his convictions.

It was hard for me to keep my mouth shut while observing this biased proceeding unfold, but there was nothing I could do as a staff person to affect the outcome. I just wished that I could have explained to the lieutenant commander afterwards that his "failure" that day had nothing to do with his personal abilities, but everything to do with his beliefs.

A more "acceptable" candidate to be a White House Fellow that year was a twenty-three-year-old ROTC graduate of Texas

A&M, named Henry Cisneros. Henry submitted his application
for a White House Fellowship a day after the deadline for submission had passed. He came to see me at our Washington
office to explain why his application wasn't in on time and to
request that we allow him to compete in the process. I was so
impressed with the young man's intelligence and maturity that
I convinced David Miller to let Cisneros enter the competition.
Thereafter, Henry sailed through the regional panel competition
and the national panel. He was awarded a White House Fellowship for the 1971-72 class. At the time I was very supportive
of his candidacy.

His assignment that year was with the secretary of HEW, Elliott
Richardson, a liberal Republican and Boston Brahmin. The liberal elite spotted a real comer in Henry and saw to it that he followed up his tenure as a White House Fellow with post-graduate
work at Harvard University. Somehow, he avoided having to fulfill
his ROTC commitment as an active duty army officer.

Henry Cisneros returned to San Antonio where he embarked on
a successful political career which led to his election as mayor
of San Antonio. In 1993 he was named by Bill Clinton as Secretary
of Housing and Urban Development. His path to political success
began with his selection as a White House Fellow. As he moved up
the ladder, he fit comfortably into that "corporate liberal" value
system so favored by the Establishment. I have listened to Henry
speak to an audience of business professionals and watched his
performance on news and public information programs. Henry
has become a very glib politician, seemingly always in step with the
"conventional wisdom" of the moment. Yet, I wonder if his beliefs
might not have turned out to be very different had he gone to
Vietnam as a young officer instead of winning a White House
Fellowship in 1971.

Repeatedly at the regional panel level, I observed Establishment
leaders and former White House Fellows recommend candidates
for the Fellowship in their own image and likeness—applicants
with an "appropriate" resumé, with a glibness that led to a good
surface impression, and an ability to feed back to the panelists
the answers they were seeking. This latter quality made it relatively easy for those selected as Fellows to adjust or modify their

views to fit the prevailing "wisdom" of the moment, whether it be in a Lyndon Johnson or a Richard Nixon administration.

The regional panels also had a built-in bias in favor of candidates with degrees from Ivy League institutions. When I was there, approximately 50 percent of those who had been White House Fellows held one or more degrees from the Ivy League schools. There were more graduates from Harvard selected than from any other college in America in those early years. This was a program for "the best and the brightest." If the cream of the Fellowship crop hadn't gotten that Ivy League exposure prior to their selection as Fellows, the liberal elite (who viewed the Fellowship program as their "baby") saw to it that they would get it afterwards—as in the case of Henry Cisneros who went to Harvard for graduate studies after his year as a White House Fellow.

This is not to say that there weren't some independent types who made it through the selection process and served as White House Fellows without letting their views be shaped by the "conventional wisdom" of the moment. I think of four in particular from the class of 1970-71: Leon (Bud) Edney, George Heilmeier, Dana Mead, and Melvin Masuda. At that time Bud was a lieutenant commander in the navy who had served with distinction in Vietnam. He was a very intelligent and disciplined career soldier with firm convictions. Later, as an admiral, Bud served as deputy chief of naval operations. Later, he was named commander in chief of the U.S. Atlantic Command.

George Heilmeier was a brilliant inventor and scientist whose patents had resulted in major technological breakthroughs in the telecommunications industry. A committed conservative, George served in the Department of Defense during his tenure as a White House Fellow, where he made major contributions to our defense systems. He remained there after his fellowship for a few years before joining Texas Instruments as its vice president of research and development. George is now president and CEO of Bellcore where he is responsible for research, development, and systems engineering for the Regional Bell operating companies.

Dana Mead is a West Point graduate and veteran of Vietnam. As a White House Fellow, Dana worked on the Domestic Affairs Council at the White House. After retiring from active duty military service, Dana Mead went into the private sector where he has been a successful business executive. Dana currently serves as a CEO of Tenneco Corporation and is the Chairman of the National Association of Manufacturers.

Mel Masuda is a Japanese-American from Hawaii who had been a journalist prior to his selection as a White House Fellow. Since we were about the same age and were both bachelors at the time, we spent a lot of time together during the Fellowship year and became good friends. He had a brilliant, analytical mind whose questions usually cut to the heart of whatever issue we were discussing. Although we didn't always agree politically, Mel Masuda impressed me as someone from the middle class who hadn't forgotten where he came from and who made up his own mind on the issues. After his Fellowship, Mel returned to Hawaii, married, and became an attorney and law professor in Honolulu.

None of these three individuals fit the typical profile of a White House Fellow. Nor did the national finalists who emerged from the New York regional panel that year. In spite of the heavy involvement of liberal Establishment types on the regional panels, we managed to achieve a few scattered victories when it came to the selection of deserving candidates. And the New York panel was a case in point. One of those who served on that panel was Neal Freeman, a successful entrepreneur and longtime associate of Bill Buckley. One of the smartest and most effective conservatives to come out of the Goldwater movement, Neal had worked with me during my tenure as College Republican chairman when he helped us raise funds after our budget had been eliminated by Ray Bliss, the Republican party chairman. Neal was an excellent judge of talent and helped ensure that the New York panel chose some excellent national finalists.

We narrowed our selection down to four recommendations for consideration as White House Fellows. One of the choices was a conservative journalist and Georgetown graduate, Frank Gannon, who had worked on a biography of Winston Churchill. Another was a female university professor who was a political refugee from the Soviet Union. The third was a successful international businessman who was a strong proponent of spurring economic growth through tax cuts. What he was advocating would later be called "supply-side" economics and would provide the philosophical underpinning for the Reagan tax cuts of 1981. The fourth choice was a New York City detective, Terry McCann. Detective McCann and Frank Gannon later were picked as White House Fellows, and I understand both men did a good job during their tenure in the Nixon administration.

One of the panelists that day was a liberal, former White House Fellow David Lelewere, who was working for the Rockefeller Foundation at the time. Lelewere had his favorite candidates who were more liberal than those ultimately selected. David Miller told me later that Lelewere had complained about the amount of influence he felt that Freeman and I had exercised over the New York panel. Needless to say, from my perspective, the best people were chosen that day.

However, this was the exception rather than the rule. Most of the Fellows were, or became, good "corporate liberals" whose views were in tune with the "politically correct" opinions of the era.

12

A Pragmatic President

"If our system does not choose the best, its winnowings tend to produce an *appropriate* man to lead us, one amenable to the merchandising trends of the moment; one who, if not really answering the needs of popular symbolism, can nonetheless be given the requisite garb or relevance. He becomes our man of the moment by accommodating the moment," said Garry Wills in *Nixon Agonistes*.

In addition to my duties with the Fellowship program, I also worked on a variety of assignments for the White House counsel, John Dean. John was the third person to serve as Nixon's principal lawyer during his first term in office. The first counsel had been John Sears, a shrewd political operative who had met the former vice president as a young attorney in the New York law firm where Nixon was a partner. Sears had been in charge of rounding up delegates for presidential candidate Richard Nixon in the 1968 primary campaign and was rewarded after Nixon's victory by being named counsel to the president. Sears, however, got crosswise with the White House chief of staff, H. R. (Bob) Haldeman, and was replaced in 1969 by a Haldeman crony, John Ehrlichman.

Ehrlichman was a Seattle lawyer who had been an advance man for Nixon in the 1968 campaign. Haldeman and Ehrlichman were close personal friends who had worked for Nixon in previous campaigns. In addition, both men were linked by a strong commitment to the Christian Science faith. In 1970 Ehrlichman moved up to run the domestic policy office at the White House, and John Dean was selected by Haldeman to be his replacement in July of that year.

At that time the top echelon of the Nixon chain of command was: Bob Haldeman, White House chief of staff; Henry Kissinger, national security adviser; John Ehrlichman, domestic policy adviser; and Charles Colson, chief political adviser. As legal counsel, John Dean reported to Bob Haldeman.

Dean was a lawyer in his early thirties who had been a deputy to Attorney General John Mitchell at the Department of Justice before joining the White House in July 1970. Shortly thereafter, David Miller introduced me to him. I began working as a staff assistant to Dean in September of that year.

The new White House counsel was very personable and easy to get along with. Only a few years older than I, he had also gone to Georgetown—I'd been an undergraduate and John was a graduate of the law school. My working for Dean was a good deal for him since my salary was being paid by the Fellowship program. It was equally advantageous to me since, if I didn't like the assignments I was given, I could simply quit and go back to working full-time at the White House Fellows office. As it turned out, I spent about half of my time working for the counsel's office that year.

It was useful for Dean to have someone like me on his staff, who had been part of the conservative movement and who had had extensive dealings with the New Left. Additionally, my military intelligence experience could come in handy as the Nixon White House wrestled with how to respond to the growing level of violence associated with the anti-Vietnam protest movement. Many federal officials saw this leftist movement as the most serious internal security threat that America had faced since the

Communist mass movements of the thirties and the Soviet spy rings and front groups in the forties and fifties.

According to Dean, when Haldeman first described the counsel's duties to him, he began by saying that: "The counsel's office would be responsible for keeping the White House informed about domestic disorders and antiwar demonstrations." I believe that John thought that I could be of assistance to him in fulfilling that particular presidential mandate.

I was twenty-six years old at the time. In Vietnam I was accustomed to seeing young men exercise a lot of responsibility. Yet it surprised me to see so many young people in key positions at the Nixon White House. Below the Haldeman-Ehrlichman-Kissinger-Colson axis at the top, the second echelon of key personnel was composed in large part of young men in their late twenties and early thirties. In addition to Dean and his chief deputy, Fred Fielding, other young White House staffers included: Fred Malek, director of White House personnel; Ron Ziegler, presidential press secretary; Jeb Magruder, deputy director of White House communications; Dwight Chapin, appointments secretary; Egil (Bud) Krogh, principal deputy to John Ehrlichman; Pat Buchanan, speechwriter; and Bill Timmons, congressional-liaison office. I didn't feel out of place on a White House staff which included so many other young people.

During the first year of the Clinton administration, many political observers commented negatively about the relative youthfulness of the Clinton White House staff. What people have tended to forget (or never realized in the first place) is that the Nixon and Clinton administrations have a lot in common in that respect. There were a lot of young people holding positions of major responsibility at the White House then.

Although I didn't know it when I went to work for him, Dean had been given a hot potato to handle by Bob Haldeman. As the new legal counsel, he was supposed to implement a domestic intelligence-gathering initiative developed by Tom Huston and known as the "Huston Plan."

A conservative activist during the sixties, Huston had been chairman of the Young Americans for Freedom (YAF) at approximately the same time that I headed the College Republicans. Now, he was on Haldeman's staff in charge of beefing up intelligence gathering on domestic organizations bent on overthrowing our government. Our intelligence agencies traditionally had focused on the dangers presented by internal subversion directed by hostile foreign governments. These "homegrown" revolutionaries were a relatively new phenomenon on the American political scene.

During this period, many of the leaders of the New Left had turned to violence to accomplish their political objectives. Certain SDS activists such as Mark Rudd decided that demonstrations and protests weren't enough any longer. They joined a more radical, underground organization known as the Weathermen and resorted to bombings and bank robberies among other activities to spur on the expected "revolution." Obviously, some members of the Left had gone beyond the rhetoric of revolution to revolutionary acts. The Nixon administration was wrestling with how to combat this new outbreak of domestic, politicized violence. The Huston Plan was one proposed solution.

When I first started working for John Dean, he waved a document at me that had been prepared by Tom Huston. Dean said that he couldn't show it to me since it required Top Secret/COMINT clearance, and my security clearance at the time was limited to Top Secret. My antenna went up since the COMINT classification was reserved for extremely sensitive information.

Dean described in general terms the parameters of the Huston Plan which would involve a much more aggressive intelligence stance directed against certain revolutionary individuals and groups in the United States. From the way John described the plan, it sounded as though Tom Huston was proposing a domestic equivalent of the CIA. Dean asked for my general views on the subject. It was one matter to be involved in covert operations targeted against hostile forces in foreign countries. The "spying" business was complicated enough, as I had discovered in Vietnam. A lot could go wrong between the planning stage of an intelligence operation and its actual execution.

I expressed my concern to Dean that anything which appeared to be akin to a domestic version of the CIA could create more problems for the administration than the ostensible benefits it would provide. The Huston Plan, as Dean described it, made me nervous. It seemed to me that there had to be a better way of beefing up the existing system of gathering information on subversive groups than creating an entirely new entity in a unilateral action by the executive branch of government. Since John already knew of my intelligence background in Vietnam and my long-standing political opposition to the New Left, he appeared somewhat surprised at my cautious response to the idea of a "domestic CIA."

What I didn't know at the time was that J. Edgar Hoover, the director of the FBI, was adamantly opposed to the Huston Plan for similar reasons. As Dean mentions in his book *Blind Ambition,* under the Huston plan, President Nixon "had ordered removal of most of the legal restraints on gathering intelligence about left-wing groups. He had authorized wiretaps, mail intercepts and burglaries.... The plan had the full support of the Central Intelligence Agency, the Defense Intelligence Agency, the National Security Agency—of everyone except Hoover's FBI. Hoover had footnoted the document with an objection that the risk of each illegal method was greater than the potential return."

During this period the administration was showing the film "The Battle of Algiers" on a regular basis to various White House aides, and arrangements were made for me to see it. This particular movie went into great detail on how the Algerian revolutionaries used bombings and other forms of urban terror to gain independence from the French. A popular training film for American radicals, "The Battle of Algiers" was used by the Nixon administration to demonstrate to its own officials how revolutionaries could resort to urban terrorism to disrupt our social and economic infrastructure.

In hindsight, all of this attention being paid to a burgeoning revolutionary movement in the United States may seem like an overreaction to insignificant fringe groups on the left. At the time, however, most Americans were unsure as to what the ultimate impact of this outbreak of leftist-inspired domestic violence would be. Riots in our major urban centers, terrorist bombings, and political kidnappings were not to be dismissed as trivial matters.

One by-product of this effort by the Nixon White House to combat leftist-generated violence was a tendency by young White

House staffers to imagine themselves "experts" in the intelligence business. This was particularly true after "The Battle of Algiers" and a few episodes of "Mission Impossible" were shown at the White House theater. It seemed as though a lot of people were running around the White House acting like "super spooks."

Following a number of conversations with John on the subject of the Huston Plan, it became clear to me that Dean was opposed to its implementation. Now, the FBI director had an ally in the White House who also had come to the conclusion that the Huston Plan had to be killed.

Dean turned to his sponsor, Attorney General John Mitchell, to carry the message to the president. As Dean describes their conversation, Mitchell was quoted as saying: "John, the president loves all this stuff, but it just isn't necessary."

The idea of a "domestic CIA" had been ended for the time being. Instead, Dean and Mitchell came up with the concept of an interagency intelligence evaluation committee which in Dean's words was "a toothless version of the Huston Plan." It was, in effect, a study group. The new proposal provided that the interagency task force would bring together under one umbrella the various intelligence organizations. Then, hopefully, these agencies would develop a more coordinated program to combat the increased threat of urban terrorism. I was Dean's representative in trying to set up this new interagency task force.

Traditionally, domestic intelligence had been the responsibility of the FBI, and I knew that J. Edgar Hoover was not open to the idea that some new organization or an interagency task force should assume responsibility for monitoring the activities of domestic subversive groups. The problem was that, while the FBI had good intelligence on black radical organizations that had turned to violence, it had been less successful in penetrating white radical groups, such as the Weathermen, who were resorting to indiscriminate bombings to "make their point." Thus, something had to be done to strengthen the intelligence collection operations against these violent organizations.

While the existing approach to dealing with this new brand of American radicalism certainly wasn't working, the Huston Plan put the administration in the position of taking unilateral executive action on a very controversial matter without seeking congressional authorization. That is why I thought that the compromise forged by John Dean was a sensible alternative to the creation of a new domestic intelligence agency. Obviously, Tom Huston wasn't pleased with the decision. Soon thereafter, he left the Nixon administration.

I hadn't anticipated that I would become involved with such sensitive issues. I have to say that I was impressed with how John Dean and Fred Fielding handled these difficult problems, particularly in light of Nixon's being so adamant about developing an aggressive "action plan" directed at these domestic revolutionary organizations. John Dean may have been very young and relatively inexperienced when he was thrust into the role of White House counsel, but he was a fast learner and a cool customer under pressure. Dean had an amazing ability to reduce various shreds of information on a particular subject to a one-page memorandum which summarized the essentials of the issue under consideration. That proved to be invaluable in a White House where decisions often were made based on written memoranda submitted by legal and policy advisers. In addition to his superior analytical skills, John had a talent for impressing his superiors. He knew how to survive and flourish in the corporation-like environment that the Haldeman-Ehrlichman faction of the Nixon administration had established.

John Dean also was shrewd enough to choose as his chief deputy a brilliant lawyer from Philadelphia, Fred Fielding, whose legal knowledge and sound political instincts complemented Dean's skills perfectly. The Dean-Fielding combination made for a winning team as they set up a first rate "law firm" for the president.

Fred and I immediately hit it off and have been good friends ever since. He impressed me from the beginning as an extremely competent lawyer with a gift for politics. Fred Fielding also possessed a character trait all too rare in the Washington political environment, particularly within the Nixon administration—Fred had a sense of personal loyalty. In a town like Washington where the prevailing attitude is aptly expressed by Don Devine, one of the original leaders of the modern conservative movement, echoing Harry Truman, "If you want a friend, get a dog," Fred Fielding remained loyal to his friends even when they were no longer in a position to be able to do anything for him.

In a way, John Dean and Fred Fielding made for an odd couple. They were different in so many ways. Yet, they both shared a high intelligence and a commitment to succeed. With Dean and Fielding in the counsel's office, they soon became known as the people to talk to if you had a problem that needed urgent attention. One of the strengths both men possessed is that they were very cool and collected when major problems erupted and other White House staffers panicked.

I saw that attribute in action when Lieutenant William Calley was convicted of murder in 1971 for his part in the My Lai massacre and was given life imprisonment by a military court. There was a public outcry against Calley's punishment, and the White House was flooded with letters and telegrams protesting his sentence. Many of the young White House aides were running around talking about how this conviction could cost Richard Nixon the election in 1972. Voices were raised, urging that the president pardon Calley immediately. I got involved in the controversy when John Dean asked me to research some of the issues relating to military law. I was impressed with how calm John remained in the midst of all this commotion.

As a result of our research on the procedures of military courts, we were able to make the case to the president's top advisers that the process of appeal of the conviction allowed for a certain amount of discretion as to a reduction of the sentence terms as well as to the reversal of the original decision. Consequently, it was the counsel's view that a presidential pardon would be a major mistake at this point in the proceedings. The advice of the White House counsel prevailed on that issue. Later, Calley's sentence was reduced, and the issue faded from public attention.

John Dean had been thrust into a difficult spot as the third White House legal counsel within the first two years of the Nixon administration. His early performance showed that he had the instincts of a political survivor in the Byzantine environment that characterized the Nixon White House. John fit the profile of the type of White House aide preferred by the Haldeman-Ehrlichman crew: he was a nonideological pragmatist.

During all the time that I worked with John, he never gave me any indication that he felt strongly about any particular political issue. He took pride in his ability to "fix" problems before they got out of hand. I accepted John's pragmatism as part of the territory that went along with his being a key player in the Nixon administration while he tolerated my more conservative views on issues. In all the time I worked for him, I don't believe that we ever had an argument.

In retrospect, Nixon clearly intended his administration to be centrist in character. To ensure this, he chose aides who did not have a firm commitment to conservative principles. The press liked to refer to the Haldeman-Ehrlichman axis as a group of "conservative" advisers. That definition fit only insofar as it reflected the personal appearance of that group. (They placed great emphasis on short haircuts and conservative dress.) It sure didn't describe their political philosophy. Purely and simply, they were technocrats—pragmatic corporate managers who could have just as easily served in a Lyndon Johnson or Jimmy Carter administration as worked for a Republican president. Take, for example, David Gergen, a Yale graduate who worked in the Nixon White House in 1971 as a speechwriter. Gergen later helped George Bush's failed Presidential campaign in 1980 and was selected by James Baker to be one of his aides in the Reagan White House. In 1993 Gergen joined the Clinton administration as a senior White House adviser.

Bob Novak correctly pegged this "corporate liberal" in a column written in *Human Events* shortly after Gergen was named to his Clinton White House post: "Gergen let it be known he had voted for Hubert Humphrey in 1968 (*when he was working for Nixon*). Positioned today as resident 'conservative' in a Democratic White House, he began as a resident 'liberal' in a Republican White House."

Haldeman was Nixon's McNamara. Called by many the assistant president, his title was chief of staff. He ran the day-to-day operations of the White House and had a major role in determining the administrative and personnel policies of the Nixon administration. A former account executive and corporate manager with the J. Walter Thompson advertising agency, Haldeman came to the White House with minimal experience in the national political arena and a limited understanding of the principal domestic and foreign policy issues that the Nixon administration would have to address. What Haldeman did bring with him was a talent for administration plus an instinct for personal survival and advancement acquired in the corporate world of advertising and public relations.

Haldeman's ascension in the Nixon White House symbolized the rise to power of corporate technocrats within the administration—men like John Ehrlichman who chaired the Domestic Affairs Council; Chuck Colson, special counsel to the president; and young appointees including Ron Ziegler, Fred Malek, and Jeb Stuart Magruder.

Nixon's national security adviser, Henry Kissinger, came out of a different milieu than most of the Nixon advisers, having been a Harvard professor and foreign policy adviser to Gov. Nelson Rockefeller. But "Henry the K," as he was called, was just as much a political pragmatist as the Haldeman crowd. Besides, as a modern disciple of Machiavelli, Henry Kissinger was one academic who knew how to use and keep power.

But there was no doubt that Haldeman was in charge at the White House. On one occasion we had a problem with the White House Fellowship program that needed his attention. I went to ask Pat Buchanan, then a White House speechwriter, about the best way to get in to see Haldeman. He thought about it for a moment and said only half in jest, "I've got it. I'll call the president and see if he can get you an appointment with him."

Haldeman was determined to run the executive branch of government as one would run a large corporation. He selected as subordinates young men strikingly out of that corporate model he prized. His own immediate staff of young aides, who always appeared to be scurrying about and shuffling papers, was dubbed the "Beaver Patrol" by less admiring members of the White House staff.

A key figure in the Haldeman operation was former management consultant, Fred Malek, who was in charge of the White House personnel office, a key position. He was known around the White House as "a young Haldeman." Although he was entrusted with the responsibility of recruiting talent for the Nixon administration, he had never been active in the Republican party. Further, he had no identifiable political philosophy other than a strong belief in corporate and material success, and was known for being impersonal and ruthless. He was a perfect choice for the job.

The principle of picking people for positions based on their material success was reflected in a letter Haldeman sent our Fellowship office, recommending that we select a young, twenty-five-year-old man as a White House Fellow because he had made a lot of money at a relatively young age. It was typical of how the Haldeman crowd measured candidates for possible appointments. Malek once complained that a particular individual should not be selected as a White House Fellow because he was over thirty years old and making only $18,000 a year.

This dominant group of corporate liberals coupled their emphasis on material success and a pragmatic value system with a barely disguised contempt for "issue-oriented" individuals, or what John Ehrlichman once referred to as "you research types." One such "issue type" was Richard Whalen, a Nixon speechwriter during the 1968 campaign.

Whalen was part of that new breed of conservative thinkers who appeared on the scene in the late fifties and early sixties. In his book *Catch the Falling Flag,* Whalen recounts how he tangled with Ehrlichman during the 1968 campaign. Ehrlichman was then in charge of "convention arrangements" and later would become the "campaign tour director." He had informed the speechwriter that he was being relegated to a secondary role and would have access to Nixon from now on only when the campaign had a specific need for his services. Whalen was more than a little miffed:

> "Just who the hell are you?" I (Whalen) asked. "I've never laid eyes on you (Ehrlichman) or heard your name mentioned. And I'll be damned if I'm going to take orders from you." "Look," (Ehrlichman) said, his own temper rising, "I've been with Nixon a long time, and I've seen writer and researcher types like you

come and go. You'll go where I say you go." "F——
you," I said, walking out. The wounding reference to
"writer and researcher types" hurt precisely because I
knew it was true. The issues men who had indeed put
their brains and pens at Nixon's disposal in former
years had indeed come and gone without a trace.

Soon thereafter, Richard Whalen would join the ranks of the
departed, and "the balloon men," as the advance men types were
called, would wind up in control of the Nixon White House.

If you had a degree from Harvard or Principia (the leading
Christian Science college), or had worked for J. Walter Thompson
Advertising Agency or McKensie and Company Management
Consultants (where Malek had worked), you had a far better
chance of getting a top job in the Nixon administration than if
you had a long-standing involvement in the battle of ideas going on
in our country.

When the Watergate crisis led to the downfall of the president,
I watched Gordon Strachen, a young White House staffer, appear
before the Watergate committee and advise young people not to go
into politics and ruin their lives. The irony was that Strachen
never really had been involved in politics. He was basically a nonpolitical type who, through his connections, had managed to land
a position in the Nixon White House and subsequently got himself
mixed up in the Watergate mess. This man, like so many others
who served in the Nixon administration, had no strong philosophical convictions.

While I never was directly involved with Chuck Colson during
my tenure in the Nixon administration, he had developed the reputation within White House circles as Richard Nixon's "hatchet
man." He took care of the dirty work for the president.

Colson was in and out of Dean's office all the time during the
period I worked for John. In one instance when I was waiting for
a meeting with John, Colson burst out of the office in a rush. I
walked in and found Dean and Fred Fielding shaking their heads.
"What's the problem?" I asked. Dean's response was that Colson
had recruited some people to skew the results of a local television station poll on Nixon's Vietnam policy.

I commented that trying to "fix" some insignificant local poll was not only a dubious enterprise for a high-level White House aide to involve himself in but that it also was the type of activity that could blow up on the perpetrators if they got caught. Dean and Fielding both thought that it was a dumb idea, but it was apparently a typical Colson scheme which he was determined to execute.

As a matter of fact, in this particular case the White House connection to the fixed poll did surface in the media with the predictable result that the administration received a lot of negative publicity. If Chuck Colson represented the "real" Richard Nixon, then perhaps my initial impression of Nixon had been correct after all. The more exposed I was to people on the White House staff, the less impressed I was with the men in charge. Other than a small group of conservatives like speechwriter Pat Buchanan, most of the young Nixon aides didn't have any real understanding of, or commitment to, the conservative philosophy. The more I observed the administration make decisions such as the imposition of wage and price controls and the preservation of LBJ's Great Society domestic spending programs, the more I concluded that the Nixon White House made policy decisions based on who squawked the loudest or what the polls suggested ought to be done.

The classic example of that mind-set was reflected in a story told me by Pat Buchanan who had just come from a meeting with John Ehrlichman, Bob Haldeman, and Ron Ziegler. The discussion concerned how the White House should handle a particularly tough issue. Buchanan was frustrated that the president's top advisers seemed concerned only with how their decision would "play in Peoria" and were not interested in the substantive arguments surrounding the disputed issue. "I wish for once," he told me, "that these guys would follow a policy because it was 'for the good of the country' rather than do what some public opinion poll tells us we should do."

The expression "for the good of the country" hit home. President Nixon and his key advisers conveyed no sense of higher purpose, no feeling that we were working for a cause greater than Nixon's reelection in 1972 and/or our own self-interest.

My reservations about the policy direction of the administration and the lack of a philosophical compass had given me second thoughts about whether I wanted to continue working for Richard Nixon. These doubts were reinforced by what Garry Wills and Richard Whalen had to say about Nixon in their respective books.

In his biography of Richard Nixon published in 1969, Wills shocked many political observers by referring to the president as a "liberal":

> Even now commentators do not see that Nixon is the authentic voice of the surviving American liberalism. They speak of his policy as a matter of zigs and zags, a welter of compromises, a muddling through the moment under prods of hope or fear. "Conservatives" (i.e., Thurmond and Mitchell) are played off against "liberals" (i.e., Finch and Moynihan), North is pitted against South....
>
> The coherence of Nixon's own views had not generally been recognized, and for an important reason: this would involve the admission that American liberalism and the emulative ethic cohere—inhere, rather, in each other. All our liberal values track back to a mystique of the earner.

I would use a slightly different term (corporate liberal) to describe the Nixon mind-set, but I found myself agreeing with Wills' basic thesis that Richard Nixon was a Wilsonian liberal.

Long before the Watergate break-in and subsequent cover-up drove Richard Nixon from the presidency, Richard Whalen was predicting that the administration was heading for a serious fall. Whalen criticized the president for failing to stand up for basic conservative principles:

> We Republicans believe in setting limits on government power and authority, as our opponents generally do not. We believe in the integrity and worth of the individual.... If we had honestly defined what was worth conserving and set about it, if we had done everything possible to turn power back toward the people (instead of merely talking about it), if we had performed the tasks government can perform well,

showing respect for the integrity of individuals, communities, and smaller nations—if we had done these
things and more, we might have rallied a cultural majority and made it an effective new political majority.

Our peril was also clear, and we have succumbed
to it. We Republicans, while temporarily enjoying gov-
erning power, have contented ourselves with overseeing a government we do not truly control, one that is
moving by blind momentum further and further away
from our party's distinctive beliefs. Without intending
it, we have replaced the meddlesome philosopher-king
of the liberal state with the repressive policeman-king
of the pseudo-conservative state. Instead of doing
everything possible to revive the decisive force for civ-
ilized order, the confidence of the people in themselves
and their freely chosen codes, we have hastened the
transformation of a free citizenry into a 'protected'
and controlled subject mass. In the process, we have
undermined our party's reason for existence.

Richard Whalen lost faith that this presidency would advance
conservative principles even before Nixon took office—as a member of his presidential campaign team in 1968.

Up until mid-1971, I had blamed the problems of the Nixon
administration on the people around the president—the Haldeman,
Ehrlichman, Colson types. I kept thinking that President Nixon
just needed better people around him, aides with strong convictions and the ability to put those principles into action. Finally, I
came to the conclusion that Dick Whalen had reached years earlier. The problem was not just with Haldeman, Ehrlichman, Malek,
or any of the other technocrats in positions of influence. The
blame rested on the man at the top who had picked the people
he wanted to run his administration. And I had no reason to
believe that things would get any better.

John Dean had offered me a new position once my commitment
to the White House Fellowship program ended. He wanted me to be
the liaison between his office and the Department of Justice in
coordinating the administration's response to internal security

problems. It meant a nice promotion for me and the opportunity to have increased responsibilities within the administration.

I had found it easy to work with John Dean. As long as you did your job, he left you alone. So I knew that, from a personal stand-point, I wouldn't have any problem in that respect. But I began to have serious reservations when I got over to the Justice Department and met some of the people I would have to work with in this new assignment. It seemed to me that everybody and his brother was getting into the act of becoming involved in the internal security issue.

Fred Malek had sent over one of his assistants, Allen May, to work on the project. May was throwing his weight around, acting like a big-shot White House aide who was determined to get his way. Although May had no experience whatsoever in the intelli-gence business, he was going to be involved in this new initiative to coordinate the intelligence agencies in combating domestic ter-rorism. Already he was acting as though he were some kind of CIA operative.

Comments by others involved in the project about what this new unit was going to do made me wonder if some folks weren't trying to put the Huston Plan back into place. I met with high-ranking officials of the FBI who were supposed to participate in this project, and it became clear to me during the course of the meeting that they were less than enthusiastic about the initiative.

I began to get the feeling that I was about to become entangled in an enterprise where I would have a lot of responsibility but very little, if any, real authority. Suddenly, I was extremely uncomfort-able about going forward in this new position and instinctively felt that something bad was going to happen if I took the job.

Not knowing what to do, I asked my good friend Fred Fielding to go to lunch with me at a small restaurant near the White House. I laid out for Fred in great detail all of the concerns I had about taking the new assignment. I felt a certain obligation to John Dean, but I no longer held the Nixon administration in high regard, as Fielding knew. In fact I had given him Dick Whalen's critical book on Nixon to read. He asked me what my alternative was, and I indicated that I had been thinking about going back to law school in Dallas. "That sounds like a good idea," Fred responded.

My decision was cinched, and I informed John Dean that I had decided to return to Southern Methodist University to get my law degree. It was the summer of 1971.

As a footnote to the story, long after I left the Nixon administration and the Watergate scandal threatened to drive from office a sitting president of the United States, I had occasion to visit George Bush who was then chairman of the Republican National Committee. It was obviously a difficult time for him. John Dean had broken with the Nixon administration and was cooperating with the Senate committee investigating the Watergate break-in and cover-up.

During my conversation with Bush, the subject of the Dean-Nixon confrontation came up; he asked me what I thought. "I think that Dean may be telling the truth," I responded. That wasn't what Bush wanted to hear, and our meeting ended shortly thereafter. But that was the way I felt at the time. It wasn't like John to get involved in something like the cover-up without acting on the orders of his superiors.

Before I returned home to Dallas, I had one final problem to contend with.

In the summer of 1971, when detente was all the rage, the White House Fellows had traveled to the Soviet Union and Eastern Europe on an education trip to meet with political leaders of the iron curtain countries. On that trip I kept a journal of my days in Moscow and the two biggest cities we visited in the Ukraine—Kharkov and Kiev. Upon returning home, those observations of mine were published in *U.S. News & World Report.* My article was clearly labeled as "personal observations" and in no way to be considered as "an official U.S. report on the trip of the White House Fellows." Prior to its publication, both Miller and an NSC official had seen what I had written and had expressed no objections to the article so long as it was identified as being my own private view.

When the article appeared in print, the Soviets went "ballistic" over it. I was denounced in the English-language edition of their newspaper, *Izvestia,* as "an outmoded Cold Warrior." The Soviet ambassador to the United States made an official protest to the U.S. government about the article and threatened never to let any future group of White House fellows visit the Soviet Union. What was all the fuss about? Apparently what upset the Soviets the most were my comments concerning the nationality problem within the USSR, the special privileges accorded the ruling Communist leaders, the unwillingness of Soviet officials to voice any public criticism about any aspect of their government, and the racial discrimination experienced by African students studying in the Soviet Union. My two concluding thoughts, I was told, also angered the Communist leaders:

1. Can the rulers of this closed society continue to keep the lid on all the internal ferment in Russia, the very existence of which they never admit, even to themselves?

2. In the West we can talk about "convergence" of our two societies, but Soviet rulers operate on an entirely different premise. Their plan for the world—to use a term that has currency among militants in the U.S.—is non-negotiable.

You would have thought from the reaction of Miller to Soviet complaints about my article that I had permanently ruined U.S.-Soviet relations all by myself. I was told that what I had written threatened the delicate relationship between our two countries.

"Was there anything substantively incorrect in what I wrote?" was my question to Miller.

"No," he replied, "I agree with most of it. It just should not have been published."

I thought to myself, "You can't tell the truth because it might damage our relationship with a totalitarian power whose interest and objectives are diametrically opposed to our own and whose propaganda apparatus regularly denounces the United States at every opportunity. This is Orwellian."

Miller was frantic in his attempts to repair the "damaged" U.S.-Soviet relationship. He was particularly worried about Soviet threats never to let the White House Fellows visit the USSR again because of my article. So Miller sent a letter of apology to the Soviet ambassador in Washington and a memorandum to all current and past White House Fellows denouncing me for writing my critique of the Soviet system. I felt the full fury of the Establishment mind-set come down on me for violating its diplomatic code, which placed a high priority on maintaining cordial relations with the Soviet empire. It took a Ronald Reagan a decade later to describe that system as it really was, "the Evil Empire."

Nearly twenty years later, I felt a certain sense of satisfaction as I sat and listened to a luncheon address in Dallas by Russian leader Boris Yeltsin, who forthrightly told his Texas audience many of those truths I had written about in 1971 but which were considered back then by our Establishment as too "provocative" for publication.

My year with the White House Fellowship program stripped away any remaining illusions that the Establishment possessed any unique skills, experience, or wisdom which made their representatives better suited than the rest of us to govern the nation. If anything, my personal exposure to Establishment leaders like Clark Clifford, Robert McNamara, David Rockefeller, John D. Rockefeller III, plus my run in with David Miller, one of their "leaders in training," convinced me that this was a bankrupt leadership class living on borrowed capital.

The problem for outsider conservatives like me and others was that, while the Establishment may have run out of ideas and no longer offered any clear vision for America, its forces still held the reins of power. Corporate liberals dominated the Washington policy-making process, the value system of big corporations, and the mind-set of the major media outlets (network news, magazines like *Time* and *Newsweek,* and newspapers like the *Washington Post* and the *New York Times).*

As I headed home, I was fully persuaded that conservatives were capable of running the federal government more effectively than the Establishment. But I doubted that we would ever have the opportunity to do so.

13

In Political Exile

Back in Dallas as a first year law student at Southern Methodist University, I intended to put the Nixon administration—and Vietnam—behind me. Easier said than done.

When the Democratic party nominated Senator George McGovern in 1972, I found myself working for Richard Nixon again, this time as a volunteer in his re-election campaign. Senator McGovern had made his opposition to the war in Vietnam the centerpiece of his campaign. In so doing, he had adopted many of the positions of the New Left, including the viewpoint that America was the real villain in that war. As much as I disliked the overall policy direction of the Nixon administration, I could not stand the thought of McGovern and his leftist allies occupying the White House.

So, in Nixon's Texas campaign, I served as the chairman of the voting bloc groups (youth, veterans, labor, Mexican-Americans, and blacks) organized to support the president. I also was a surrogate speaker for the campaign. In that latter role, I debated various McGovern representatives. One of those opponents turned out to be a young lawyer and former anti-Vietnam activist named Jim Mattox whom I would later tangle with in two bitterly fought congressional races.

It was an easy sell, convincing people to vote against McGovern. Richard Nixon won a resounding victory in November, 1972, and I headed back to my books.

I finished my course work in two and a half years and took my bar exam in the spring of 1974. While waiting for the test results, I went to Corpus Christi for a vacation. There, I met my wife, Ida Ayala. It was one of those whirlwind romances, and we married that summer. Twenty years (and seven children) later, I still consider myself fortunate that circumstances brought us together.

Having passed the bar exam, I hung out my law shingle in a small office in East Dallas. My wife and I lived in a duplex apartment above the office. Although it was a struggle at first, I was making real headway in building my legal practice by 1975 when our first son was born.

Then everything changed.

Dramatic events had altered the political landscape from the time of Nixon's re-election in 1972 to that unforgettable day in the spring of 1975. I watched on the sidelines as the Democratically controlled Congress turned against the war. The burgeoning Watergate crisis had weakened the Nixon presidency in its second term. Beginning in 1973, Congress substantially reduced military aid to our South Vietnamese allies as the remaining American troops were withdrawn from Vietnam. When the Watergate scandal forced Richard Nixon to resign from the presidency in 1974, he was succeeded in office by Vice President Gerald Ford. Congressional Democrats made huge gains in the November elections that year. The handwriting was on the wall. North Vietnamese forces stepped up their military attacks on the South in early 1975. In March, 1975, Congress refused to provide $300 million in needed military aid to enable the South Vietnamese government to withstand the North Vietnamese military offensive. The end was near.

Saigon fell to the Communists in April, 1975. I sat glued to our television set at our small home in East Dallas watching NBC newsman Jack Perkins report from Saigon. North Vietnamese troops marched triumphantly into the capital city of South Vietnam. It was one of the worst sensations I have ever had, comparable to how I felt when I learned of the assassination of President John F. Kennedy. There was an empty feeling in the pit of my stomach. I was furious at what I was seeing live on the screen. It seemed to me as though the tone of Perkins' voice was almost gleeful as he described the events surrounding the Communist victory in Vietnam. Henceforth, Saigon would be known as Ho Chi Minh City. I remember cursing at what I saw on the screen and being outraged that this American newsman on the scene seemed so cavalier about what was happening.

It is hard for Americans who weren't there to understand how traumatic that event was for those of us who served. Other than the Vietnamese themselves, two and a half million American soldiers were the most affected by this longest war in our history. This "protracted struggle," as North Vietnam's leading strategist Truong Chinh put it, claimed the lives of more than 57,000 Americans and hundreds of thousands of South Vietnamese. And all for this? When the end came, only a small contingent of American advisers were still in Vietnam. But the defeat was still a particularly bitter pill to swallow.

I realized that this was a war that was managed by politicians and lost by politicians. Realizing how much politicians can influence our lives, I made up my mind to do all I could to change the leadership of our country.

In one way or another, I have been active in politics ever since. In 1976 I challenged an incumbent Democratic state senator, Bill Bracklein, and lost by approximately eight hundred votes out of more than a hundred thousand cast. Two years later I was the Republican nominee running against Jim Mattox, the incumbent Democratic congressman from the Fifth District in Texas. Mattox and I had squared off before when he was the chief spokesman for the McGovern campaign in 1972. He was a formidable opponent who had gotten his start in politics as part of the anti-Vietnam protest movement in the late sixties. In 1976 Jim Mattox had been elected to Congress, and he was known as a tireless campaigner who would do whatever it took to win. He maximized the advantages of being an incumbent congressman, using his free mailings (known as the franking privilege) to blanket the district with materials informing the voters what a "great job" he was doing for them. In addition, as a member of the House Banking Committee, he was effective in "encouraging" the banking and Savings & Loan communities to provide substantial contributions to his campaign. Political experts viewed my prospects of unseating Mattox as somewhere between slim and none. That was before Ronald Reagan came into the district to campaign for me in the spring of 1978.

I had followed Reagan's career as he sought to win the Republican presidential nomination, first in 1968 and more seriously in 1976 when he narrowly lost the nomination to the incumbent Republican president, Gerald Ford. Nonetheless, Reagan kept plugging along on behalf of the conservative cause in spite of his personal setbacks. In 1978 he traveled the country on behalf of Republican candidates for Congress. I was one of the people he helped.

When he came to Garland, Texas, to campaign for me in my race against Mattox, I sensed that Ronald Reagan might some day be elected president of the United States. An incredible number of people turned out that spring evening at the Holiday Inn ballroom to listen to the leader of the American conservative movement. Many more were turned away because there simply was no more room inside.

We were afraid the fire marshal was going to shut us down, but fortunately he was a Reagan enthusiast too, and worked with us to allow the event to go forward. There was an electricity in the air which was difficult to describe.

Barry Goldwater had used the term "forgotten Americans" in his 1964 campaign to describe middle class, working people whose voices weren't being heard by Washington politicians and bureaucrats. Ronald Reagan spoke for these unrepresented Americans that evening, and an army of committed citizens left the hall willing to do whatever it took to elect Ronald Reagan.

A brief personal footnote to the Reagan visit—in the midst of all the bedlam and the crowd adulation, Ronald Reagan displayed a personal graciousness toward my wife and parents that said something about his character. By 1978, I had been around enough politicians to have developed a pretty cynical attitude toward most of them. Too many of them seemed motivated primarily by ego gratification and a quest for power. Reagan was different. Not only was he a solid conservative, but he came across to me and my family that evening as a man of good character. That "gut" feeling about Ronald Reagan has stuck with me over the years.

I had another disappointing close call that year, losing to Mattox in November by some eight hundred votes. I was beginning to feel that my determination to make a difference on the American political scene was going to come to naught.

While many sixties generation conservatives like me had remained active politically, our counterparts on the left also were hard at work trying to influence the political direction of the country. Tom Hayden moved to California, married the well-known actress and political activist Jane Fonda, and organized a grassroots political movement in that state called the Campaign for Economic Democracy. Within a few short years, this remnant of the New Left had become a potent political force, helping to elect Jerry Brown governor of California in 1974.

But one problem for the New Left was that it had not been able to seize a political issue with the kind of mass appeal Vietnam had. In late 1978 Hayden thought that he had found just such an issue in the controversy over the building of nuclear power plants in the United States. An accident in the Three Mile Island nuclear plant near Harrisburg, Pennsylvania, in 1979 had set off an outpouring of public concern about the safety of American nuclear power facilities.

Hayden was quick to take advantage of these fears of a "nuclear accident" by organizing a fifty city tour across the country to warn of the dangers of nuclear power and to build a major political movement around the antinuclear issue. Jane Fonda was Hayden's featured attraction to garner publicity and crowds for the tour.

Months before the antinuclear campaign began, I was sitting at home in Texas when I saw Tom Hayden quoted on television, saying that he and his group were right to warn of the dangers of nuclear energy just as they had been right in their criticism

SHELBYVILLE-SHELBY COUNTY
PUBLIC LIBRARY

of the Vietnam War. Hayden also boasted that the next generation of U.S. political leaders would come from the ranks of
the anti-Vietnam activists, as opposed to the situation after
World War I and World War II when those who had served went
on to lead this country.

What Hayden said made me angry. From my perspective, he
was dead wrong in claiming that his views on Vietnam had been
vindicated. I was furious at the major media for letting him get
away with these blanket assertions. Granted, the New Left had
won the political battle over Vietnam in the media and even in
Congress after the Democratic landslide of 1974. Moreover,
Hayden's side had won the war, as we could observe on television
in 1975 when North Vietnamese troops triumphantly marched
into Saigon. But Hayden and his fellow New Left activists were
dead wrong in their claims that an allied defeat in South Vietnam
would benefit the people of Indochina. The human tragedy that
followed the Communist takeover of Vietnam is an undisputed
fact of history. We now know about the "re-education" camps in
South Vietnam for opponents of the Communist regime; about
the flight of the boat people escaping from Vietnam; about the
mass genocide committed against the Cambodian people by the
Communist Khmer Rouge regime; and about the dropping of
poisonous "Yellow Rain" on the Meong tribesmen in Laos by the
Communist rulers there.

As for Hayden's assertion that the New Left would provide
America with its next generation of political leaders, my reaction
was that I would do what I could to prevent that from happening.
Shortly thereafter, I set about to make a documentary film on the
New Left's exploitation of the nuclear issue for political gain.

Previously, I had worked with two documentary filmmakers
from Dallas, Zack Burkett and John Rudin, on a successful pro-
motional film for Tuskegee Institute entitled "Because They Care."
So I contacted Zack and John to see if they would be willing to
work with me on a film about the New Left's sudden fascination
with the nuclear issue. They were agreeable to the idea, and I
went about raising the money to make the film. Some committed
Dallas businessmen, including my good friend Bill Bowen (a successful venture capitalist whom I would go to work for after

leaving the Reagan administration) contributed to our efforts. I was able to secure just enough funds to pay for the hard costs of the film, our equipment, location shooting, editing, and the purchase of necessary film footage.

The documentary traced the activities of the New Left from the anti-Vietnam era to its current involvement in nuclear energy. The film distinguished between those who opposed the war for legitimate reasons (including pacifists like Joan Baez who opposed all wars) and those who openly and actively supported the victory of the Viet Cong and the North Vietnamese. The most graphic supporting evidence for our viewpoint was uncovered by our director Zack Burkett in the archives of UPI-TN, a film library housed in an old warehouse building in New York City.

The particular film clip featured Jane Fonda sitting on an anti-aircraft gun in North Vietnam, with an ecstatic look on her face as she participated viscerally in the "struggle against the American imperialists." That footage of Jane Fonda in North Vietnam, shown in conjunction with an interview of former POW and Medal of Honor winner Colonel George Day, who, as a POW in a Communist prison camp, was forced to watch Jane Fonda in Hanoi, helped explain why so many of us were still bitter years later over the conduct of certain prominent Americans of our generation during that war.

The film title "Whatever Works" was a phrase used by syndicated columnist Robert Novak, one of the people we interviewed for the documentary. As the narrator of the film, I had asked Novak if he thought that the nuclear power issue would be as effective politically for the New Left in the eighties as Vietnam had been in the sixties and early seventies. Novak felt (correctly, as it later turned out) that the nuclear energy question just didn't have the kind of mass appeal that would allow the left to mobilize large numbers of Americans on an ongoing basis against its use. Consequently, from Novak's perspective, once the nuclear issue failed to help the Left achieve greater political power, the activists would go onto other issues until they found one that clicked with the American public.

In Novak's words, the New Left would use "whatever works." When he said those words, I knew we had our title. One thing I had learned in my extensive exposure to the views of sixties radicals: issues are political weapons to be used to gain political power. If one works, keep using it so long as it helps to advance the political objectives of the movement. If the issue doesn't achieve the desired results, then drop it and move on to something else that has more potential to arouse public indignation.

We were able to finish our film just prior to the launching of the antinuclear campaign in Harrisburg, near Three Mile Island. Prior to the start of the tour, the antinuclear forces were able to generate a significant amount of favorable publicity in the mainstream media.

So Zack Burkett and I headed to Pennsylvania to preview our film to coincide with the Hayden-Fonda tour kickoff. Through an incredible coincidence, the Pennsylvania American Legion was holding a state conference on the same day and at the same hotel where Hayden and Fonda planned to announce the beginning of their antinuclear tour later that evening.

The first showing of our film was at the Legionaries convention that afternoon. I paid close attention to the reaction of the audience because it was the first time that an outside group had seen our film; we weren't quite sure what kind of a response it would receive.

Immediately, I could tell that the segment dealing with Vietnam had a powerful and immediate impact on the audience. The picture of Jane Fonda on that anti-aircraft gun in Hanoi combined with hard evidence that Hayden, Fonda, and others had defended the actions of our enemy in Vietnam affected the audience. Without any encouragement from us, the veterans on their own decided to picket the Hayden and Fonda event. They prepared handmade signs which they carried in protest that evening. The major media covered the veterans' demonstration, and the debate finally had been joined. From that moment on, Tom Hayden and Jane Fonda were forced to answer questions from the media about their actions.

From there, Hayden and Fonda went to Washington, D.C., for a major address before the prestigious National Press Club. Again, we timed our appearance to preview our film for reporters prior to their luncheon speech. We rented a small room at the

Press Club that morning. Colonel George Day had joined us in Washington to answer questions from the media after the showing of the documentary. He described what it was like as a prisoner of war to see American leftists like Jane Fonda and Tom Hayden being used for propaganda purposes by their North Vietnamese captors.

I had to chuckle over the irony of our circumstances. Two prominent figures associated with the sixties counterculture were guests of honor at a major luncheon event hosted upstairs by the most prestigious media organization in America while our small band of conservatives (Zack Burkett, Bud Day, and I) were scrambling frantically to get some of the members of the Washington press corps to cover the preview of a documentary film rebutting the Hayden view of the war and nuclear power. I felt as though I were part of a new counterculture.

We were pleasantly surprised when a packed room of reporters showed up to view "Whatever Works." Our documentary film traced the activities of the New Left from its anti-Vietnam origins to its involvement in the antinuclear movement.

Once the film was over, we were bombarded with questions. A few journalists who clearly didn't like the message of our film sought to find factual errors in order to discredit the documentary. We had gone to great lengths to carefully document our claims, particularly those relating to the conduct of the youthful radicals during the Vietnam War. As a result, these efforts to discredit the film failed. Other reporters were taken aback by some of the disclosures concerning Hayden and Fonda's activities during the war. They simply could not explain away or justify the actions of Jane Fonda, sitting in the cockpit of a North Vietnamese anti-aircraft gun which was used to shoot down American planes. That visual picture of her in that setting was (to borrow a cliche) more powerful than thousands of words. I could tell from the reaction that Fonda and Hayden would be forced to explain their actions when the question and answer period took place after their speeches to the National Press Club.

That is exactly what happened. Ms. Fonda was unable to offer a satisfactory explanation for her behavior, either then or thereafter in other cities along the fifty-city tour.

Within a few weeks after the initial kickoff campaign in Harrisburg, the antinuclear campaign of Hayden and Fonda began to lose steam. Their past activities caught up with the twosome. In fact, Jane Fonda received so much criticism for her support of Communist North Vietnam that she dropped out of the Hayden-directed road show before it ended.

Clearly, our efforts to set the record straight about their conduct in that war led to the less than favorable reception from the American public to their fifty-city antinuclear campaign. The Hayden-Fonda tour ultimately fizzled out. It never attracted broad-based support. Ms. Fonda later issued an apology of sorts for her conduct in Vietnam. To my knowledge, Tom Hayden has yet to admit that what he did during the war was wrong.

In this particular instance, we won an important victory for our side in the continuing battle to define the meaning of Vietnam.

Meanwhile, on the political front, I continued my record of near misses, losing another close election to Jim Mattox in 1980. But, out of that defeat, there came a terrific consolation prize— the opportunity to join the "Reagan Revolution." Thanks to my good friend Fred Fielding, who was serving as Reagan's legal counsel during the transition period between the November victory and the January inaugural, I was asked to join the Reagan transition team as it prepared to assume control of the executive branch of government.

14

Transition: Liberal Roadblocks

It was an exciting moment—we conservatives were coming to Washington to dismantle the modern liberal state.

I began work in the legal counsel's office, helping to clear Reagan appointees who had been selected to serve in the new administration and who had to go through the legal clearance process prior to their names being forwarded to the Senate for confirmation.

Our job in the counsel's office was to make sure that there weren't any conflicts between the private business interests of the nominees and their new public responsibilities. In addition, Fred Fielding would examine the FBI background investigation on each nominee to determine if there were any serious problems which might disqualify a candidate from serving in a high level federal position. Also, he would review financial records to make sure that the candidate didn't have any current or past tax problems. If everything checked out, we would interview each candidate to try to ferret out any other possible impediments to the appointment. It was better to know all of the potential problems ahead of time, prior to having them surface in the press or before a Senate committee—as Bill Clinton later found out with the nomination of Zoe Baird for attorney general.

Under our constitutional system, while the president can nominate whomever he wants to serve in what are called "executive level" positions, the Senate has the authority to approve or reject his nominees. A nominee's prospective career hangs in the balance. Once confirmed, a presidential appointee can be removed from office only for cause; he remains in that post unless the President removes him or he decides to leave the position voluntarily.

In *Advise and Consent,* the political thriller by Allen Drury, a reporter who covers the congressional beat describes a bitter fight between members of the Senate and the president over whether to confirm a controversial presidential nominee as secretary of state.

The most notable actual confirmation battles in recent years were over the Supreme Court Justice nominations of Robert Bork and Clarence Thomas. Liberal activists did their best to deny these two men seats on the judicial body. They succeeded in blocking Bork's appointment but failed to muster enough votes to defeat Thomas.

Until Ronald Reagan became president, the scenario laid out by Allen Drury was a rare exception in the process of senatorial approval of presidential nominees. Instead, the common practice in recent decades was for the Senate to approve the appointments of the president with little or no debate. The nominee's name would be forwarded to the particular Senate committee which had jurisdiction over the agency or department where the appointee would serve. A hearing would be scheduled for the nominee to appear before the committee. The nominee generally would be introduced by a Senator from his own state and then would read his statement to the committee as to what he hoped to accomplish in his new post. Then, the Senate committee would vote to approve the nomination and forward it to the full Senate.

These formalities suddenly changed when Ronald Reagan decided to appoint conservatives. It was one thing to have to put up with a conservative in the White House, but something else to have a bunch of "Reaganauts" running the various agencies and departments.

Liberal Democrats in the Senate, in close collaboration with their ideological soul mates in the media, quickly developed strategies to derail the nominations of "right-wingers" they found particularly offensive. The liberals were going to show the new president who was "boss."

Even though Republicans held a narrow majority in the Senate in 1981, liberal Democrats remained a potent force, and could count on a few "progressive" Republicans to join them in such battles.

Their first targets were Ray Donovan, secretary of labor-designate; James Watt, secretary of the interior-designate; and William Clark, deputy secretary of state-designate. These three men had a couple of things in common—they had supported Ronald Reagan from the beginning, and they were solid conservatives. So, they became immediate targets. After difficult confirmation battles, however, all three were confirmed. Ronald Reagan had survived his first test of wills with the liberals in Congress.

Conservatives' problems weren't just limited to congressional liberals' trying to prevent Ronald Reagan from appointing conservatives to execute his policies. There were deep divisions within the Reagan transition team itself over the question of political appointments.

The man named to head the White House personnel operation, during both the transition and the early years of the Reagan administration, was Pendleton (Pen) James who was viewed by Reagan conservatives as little more than a Nixon retread. He was non-ideological and had served in the personnel shops of the Nixon and Ford administrations. James's chief deputy, James Cavanaugh, had been chief of staff to Vice President Nelson Rockefeller during the Ford administration. Cavanaugh ran the day-to-day operations of the personnel transition office. Conservatives were appalled at the thought of a Rockefeller Republican recommending who should staff a Reagan administration.

The principal argument that the James-Cavanaugh group made in recommending many of their old friends and associates for jobs in the new administration was that, unlike Reagan conservatives who were "too inexperienced" for major appointments, they had the credentials and the experience to handle these difficult assignments. In some instances, their position was valid. You don't want an inexperienced person running the CIA. In that particular instance, the president picked his campaign chairman, Bill Casey. Casey had been an experienced OSS intelligence operative during World War II and later served in the Nixon administration as chairman of the Securities and Exchange Commission.

But many of the people James and Cavanaugh were promoting had held low- to mid-level posts in the Nixon and Ford administrations. Moreover, few of them could be classified as Reagan Republicans. Not only had they not done anything to help elect Reagan president, many of them had been openly contemptuous of Reagan for years, viewing him as just another "right-wing nut."

Conservatives were furious. While his supporters had been enthusiastically celebrating victory, pragmatic Republicans were busy shaping his new administration by putting their allies into key positions. Perhaps we weren't sophisticated or experienced enough to realize that the battle had just begun and that it wasn't just liberal Democrats who feared a conservative administration. A lot of Republicans were nervous about this right-wing, shoot-from-the-hip westerner coming to power. They wanted to ensure that "wiser" heads would prevail in staffing this new administration and deflect it from pursuing Reagan's conservative agenda.

Working in the counsel's office, I saw the selection process being manipulated to our detriment. Typically, three names were submitted to the Reagan hierarchy as finalists for appointment to the various openings. The appointee could be named from among those choices. While this system seemed to make sense procedurally, outstanding candidates (who happened to be conservatives) would often simply be left off the final list by the James-Cavanaugh clique. Two of the names sent forward by the personnel office for consideration would be unsuitable candidates for various reasons, leaving only one real choice for the Reagan hierarchy to consider. That just happened to be the person preferred by the Cavanaugh group. A lot of good conservatives were kept off that final list in order to smooth the way for "pragmatic" Republicans to serve in a "conservative" administration.

Fortunately for Reagan conservatives, Lyn Nofziger rejoined the transition team in early December. He had been one of Ronald Reagan's closest political associates for many years. He was also Reagan's principal link to the conservative political leaders, virtually all of whom knew and trusted him.

I had known Lyn since my College Republican days when he was a political reporter for the *San Diego Union-Tribune,* and held him in high regard. I think that most conservatives who knew Lyn would say the same—he was a political loyalist from the old school who had an institutional knowledge not only of those who had helped Reagan but also of those Republicans who had tried to prevent Ronald Reagan from reaching the White House.

Lyn immediately went to work to ensure that conservatives got a fair shake. Thereafter, a much higher percentage of conservatives were nominated for presidential appointments, due in no small part to Lyn Nofziger's bulldog-like commitment to straighten out the personnel selection process.

James Cavanaugh was gone within a few weeks and the internal bickering between conservatives and Republican pragmatists became less pronounced. But the administration paid a heavy price for losing control over its personnel selection process during this early stage. A number of those appointed to run agencies and departments did not truly believe in the Reagan agenda. This caused the President significant problems when it came time to implement his program.

Thus, a conservative president was often forced to rely for the implementation of his conservative agenda on people who, more often than not, were centrist, pragmatic Republicans. In light of this "bloodless coup," it is not surprising that many of Reagan's policy initiatives were scuttled or altered beyond recognition.

Like many conservatives, I had my own difficulties with the James-Cavanaugh personnel operation. I had asked to be considered for the position of director of ACTION. ACTION is a relatively obscure federal agency whose mission is to encourage voluntarism through such federally-assisted volunteer programs as the Retired Senior Volunteer Program (RSVP), Foster Grandparents,

Senior Companions, Volunteers in Service to America (VISTA), and (at the time) the Peace Corps.

Although the Peace Corps was officially under the umbrella of ACTION when Ronald Reagan took office in 1981, the Peace Corps's had its own director and was semi-autonomous. There had been a lot of friction during the Carter years between Sam Brown, the director of ACTION, and the director of the Peace Corps, over who had the final say with respect to Peace Corps operations.

The Reagan administration was hoping to rectify that organizational conflict by making the ACTION director responsible for all domestic and foreign volunteer initiatives. This effectively would put the director of ACTION in charge of the Peace Corps as well as VISTA and the senior volunteer programs.

The ACTION job was attractive to me for a number of reasons. First, I would have the opportunity to manage an agency plagued with problems throughout the seventies. Brown was undoubtedly the most controversial individual to head ACTION since its establishment as an independent agency in the early seventies. He had been one of the leaders of the anti-Vietnam movement during the sixties and had turned ACTION into a playpen for New Left activists during the Carter years. In addition to staffing the agency with political appointees who shared his ideological commitment to a radical restructuring of American society, Brown used federal dollars earmarked for VISTA to fund what seemed like virtually every remnant of the New Left apparatus remaining from the turbulent sixties.

I figured that if I were put in charge of the agency by President Reagan, I had enough experience battling the New Left crowd over the years to undo the damage that Brown had done at ACTION.

Second, it seemed to me that running a small agency like ACTION would allow for greater leeway to develop and test alternative ways of delivering social services with the dual objective of spending fewer tax dollars and accomplishing more good for those in need. The Great Society programs weren't working. Surely, there was a better way to improve the social condition of the poor.

Additionally, overseeing the Peace Corps would allow me to become involved in the foreign policy arena, which had intrigued me ever since my Georgetown University days—more so after my

Vietnam experience. I thought that Ronald Reagan was the first President since John F. Kennedy to understand the importance of national symbols in conveying the spirit of America to the rest of the world.

The Peace Corps had been one of Kennedy's most recognizable symbols. But the 1980s were not the 1960s, and to many of us, the Peace Corps seemed frozen in time. The new Peace Corps strategy reflected the different era we lived in and the Reagan philosophy of encouraging social and economic entrepreneurship. I would enjoy that kind of challenge.

Finally, I sought the ACTION job for a very practical reason. Given my background and experience, it was a position within the administration for which I could qualify and which I considered attainable. My political involvement as a Goldwater-Reagan conservative dated back to my college days, and I received the endorsement of those who wanted a solid conservative to replace Sam Brown. Having previous experience in a Republican administration and having run a strong race for Congress against an incumbent Democrat also strengthened my candidacy. But, what really allowed me to be a serious contender for the ACTION post was the active support of many friends with close ties to the incoming administration.

There was only one minor problem—the word was out that Jim Cavanaugh had "earmarked" the job for a moderate Republican friend of his who worked for Senator John Danforth of Missouri. So our first task was to make sure that I wasn't eliminated from the competition in the early stages of the process. My first problem was that my resumé kept getting "lost" over in the personnel shop. With a handy copy machine available, I would duplicate another one and send it over again. After a while, my disappearing resumé became a standing joke among my friends. It is a lot funnier now than it was at the time; but, had I not been on the Reagan transition team with friends on the inside, my name never would have surfaced at the senior staff level as a prospective candidate for ACTION director.

At that time, I still enjoyed a good relationship with Vice President-elect George Bush and incoming chief of staff James Baker, and their support proved very helpful.

At last the day came when the names of the finalists were forwarded to the senior staff for the final decision. I had been told that I had made the final cut, but my hopes were dashed when a friend in the know informed me that someone named "Plunkett" had been named to head ACTION. The only person my friend Alex Armandaris could think of with that name was Jim Plunkett, the pro football quarterback. I thought that this was a heck of a note, to lose out to a sports celebrity whose name had never been mentioned in all the discussions about possible candidates. As it turned out, however, somebody had gotten my name confused and transposed Pauken into Plunkett. I got the call that evening from (of all people) Jim Cavanaugh, informing me of the president's intent to nominate me as director of ACTION. I had made it through the first stage of the process.

But, as I soon found out, I would have to postpone celebrating. To be nominated is not enough; one also must be confirmed. My conservative reputation had preceded me, and my name must have shown up on the liberal "radar screen" as a "target of opportunity." In particular, the very fact of my nomination incensed Democratic Senator Alan Cranston of California, one of the most ideologically-minded leftists in the U.S. Senate.

When President Carter had named Sam Brown to head ACTION, Senator Cranston declared that it was "another remarkable nomination of the president" and that Brown was an "outstanding young American." When my name surfaced as Reagan's pick to replace Brown, Cranston began mobilizing opposition in the Senate to my appointment. He assigned his top aide, Jonathan Steinberg, to coordinate the campaign to defeat my nomination.

Steinberg was a shrewd Capitol Hill operative who had been a hard-core, anti-Vietnam activist back in the old days. Both Steinberg and Cranston had close ties to New Left leaders like Tom Hayden and Sam Brown, and my nomination to head ACTION was not welcome in those circles.

Bob Shrum, my old classmate from Georgetown, happened to be Senator Ted Kennedy's speechwriter at the time and was at a party with Sam Brown when Brown learned that I had been named to take his place. According to Shrum, Brown's response was, "Oh no, not that f——g fascist." I am sure that our 1979 film on the New Left, "Whatever Works," had more than a little to do with Sam's reaction and the subsequent leftist campaign to defeat my nomination.

Steinberg was an excellent choice to head up the effort to defeat my nomination. A well-connected Washington insider, he wielded so much influence within Senator Cranston's office that some reporters had begun referring to the senator as Senator Cranberg.

Steinberg was one of those behind-the-scenes operators who wield such enormous influence in Washington. His role as Senator Cranston's staff representative on the Senate Veterans Committee and the Senate Foreign Relations Committee gave him the opportunity to mold legislation, determine how money would be allocated within certain executive agencies and departments, and influence the type of relationship the agency or department head would enjoy with the committee that had oversight over the agency. It was an incredible amount of power to bestow on someone who had never been elected and who was a virtual unknown to anyone outside the Washington Beltway.

Steinberg took advantage of the virtual carte blanche authority given him by Senator Cranston to develop a well-deserved reputation as one of the most feared aides on Capitol Hill. By 1981, he actually wielded more political power than some senators and congressmen.

What made my problem even more difficult was that Steinberg was a "true believer." His political involvement apparently dated from his anti-Vietnam activism in the sixties and early seventies. According to people who were at the Peace Corps at the time that Steinberg was working as a lawyer in the general counsel's office, he helped organize a highly visible protest of Peace Corps employees against Nixon's policies on Vietnam. The demonstration was a public relations coup for the antiwar movement at the time.

From Steinberg's perspective, I must have been the worst possible choice to succeed Sam Brown. He obviously had a special interest in what went on at the Peace Corps, having worked there as a lawyer during the Vietnam War and did not want me anywhere near the place. Moreover, Steinberg was one of those Hill aides who try to micromanage agencies over which their bosses enjoy oversight authority. One good way to micromanage an agency is to make sure you can work with whoever is in charge. We both knew that wouldn't happen if I was confirmed as ACTION director.

The great advantage that the Left has over conservatives in our ongoing political warfare is its dominance of the mainstream media. The practical reality is that an overwhelming percentage of the working press who cover politics hold liberal political views. Many try to maintain an objectivity in their coverage of both sides of controversial issues, but others barely disguise their advocacy of a leftist political agenda. Moreover, it is difficult for the public to sort out what is fair coverage and what is clearly biased when it comes to stories on politics and political personalities. These factors combine to put conservatives at a decided disadvantage in communicating their views through the media.

The liberal hive quickly went to work "defining" me—utilizing their contacts in the media to frame the debate on my nomination. One Washington columnist reported that I had been involved in efforts in Texas to create an all black congressional district. It sounded from the tone of the article as if I favored a South African style of racial separatist politics. The truth was that, as an attorney, I had represented a group of black citizens in Dallas County who were concerned that redistricting lines were being drawn to benefit white liberal Democrats to the detriment of minority candidates.

After reading the article, Lowell Weicker, then a Republican senator from Connecticut, was prepared to vote against my nomination until I was able to meet with him personally and explain. (If you don't think the media has the ability to influence the opinions of supposedly sophisticated people, just imagine yourself in a situation where you are trying to defend your reputation from a story about you that bares little relationship to the truth.)

By the time I was able to clear up these misrepresentations, a new canard appeared in the media to derail my nomination. "Covert Agent in ACTION" was the headline of a story in Philip Agee's leftist publication entitled *Covert Action*.

Agee was a disaffected CIA agent who had gone over to the Left, and now edited a magazine which sought to blame the CIA for virtually everything bad going on in the world. According to the article in question, I had been a CIA operative in Vietnam and was part of an agency effort to take over the Peace Corps and turn it into a CIA front.

Soon, other articles appeared in international publications maintaining that the lives of Peace Corps volunteers would be threatened because of my intelligence background in Vietnam. According to this line of attack, my appointment as director of ACTION would be seen by many as a sign that the Reagan administration was turning the Peace Corps into an arm of American intelligence.

I received a call from Larry O'Brien, Jr., with whom I had served in Vietnam and whose father had been chairman of the Democratic National Committee. Larry told me that someone from Cranston's office had called, asking him for information that might connect me with the CIA during my Vietnam service as well as any information that might link me to the Phoenix program. O'Brien told me that he had explained that, as far as he knew, I had not worked for the CIA in Vietnam or been involved with the Phoenix program. But, according to Larry, his answers had failed to satisfy Cranston's representative. The witch hunt was on.

My nomination was forwarded in early February to the Senate Labor and Human Resources Committee headed by Republican Senator Orrin Hatch of Utah. It had the authority to approve or reject presidential appointees for ACTION. I did not anticipate any problems so I assumed my name could go forward to the full Senate for confirmation fairly quickly. Even Senator Ted Kennedy, the ranking Democrat on the committee, informed me privately that he had no opposition to my nomination. Cranston and my former congressional opponent Jim Mattox had tried to get Kennedy to lead the fight against me, but my good friend and former classmate Bob Shrum was kind enough to convince the senator that I was not a bad guy "for a right-winger." Besides, as Shrum explained to me, the senator didn't want to lead the fight against the appointment of a Vietnam veteran to a high position.

Thus, it appeared at first glance that I had dodged the several political bullets fired my way by the liberal hive. I sailed through the Senate Labor and Human Resources Committee with minimal opposition. But Senator Cranston argued that, since the Peace Corps was still under ACTION, I must also face the Senate Foreign Relations Committee where Cranston was a high-ranking member. At the time, the committee was chaired by Republican Senator Charles Percy of Illinois whom I had listened to on the steps of the Capitol some eleven years earlier as he tried to appease both sides on the issue of Vietnam. Now, my fate was in his hands, and he appeared to be trying to have it both ways with respect to my nomination.

I met with Senator Percy and explained to him that this business of making me go before the Senate Foreign Relations Committee was simply a tactic that Cranston was using to delay and defeat my nomination. I pointed out that my predecessor Sam Brown was required to go before only one committee, although the Peace Corps was part of ACTION then. Why should I be treated differently? None of what I had to say made any difference to Senator Percy. He assured me that I didn't have anything to worry about and that I had his "full support," even as he acceded to Cranston's request.

At the same meeting, we discussed my military intelligence activities in Vietnam. I expressed no objection to Percy examining my military records, although I explained to the senator that my work in Vietnam was of a secret nature and that I felt a responsibility not to disclose the full extent of those activities. I emphasized that those records should be for his review only and should not be given to Cranston's office. He agreed to maintain the strict confidentiality of the records.

I left Percy's office that day very concerned about my ability to win approval from the committee, a committee whose makeup was more liberal than that of the Senate Labor and Human Resources Committee. I couldn't even be assured of full Republican support, being particularly concerned that I would lose the Republican votes of Senators Charles "Mac" Mathias of Maryland and Rudy Boschwitz of Minnesota. I had little confidence in Senator Percy's "soothing" words of comfort.

With help from my good friend John Ryan who had worked as a legislative aide to Republican Senator Harrison Schmidt, I put together a working group to try to salvage the nomination. I went to see Senator Mathias, one of the most liberal Republicans in the Senate and a man not likely to support a conservative like me to head ACTION. The senator and I got along well in our initial meeting, and more important, a woman on his staff waded in heavily on my behalf with her boss.

"Why should this man be penalized for having served his country as an intelligence officer in Vietnam?" she asked. She went on to say that many good people had worked for our country in the intelligence business and that such service should not be an impediment to government appointment. I am convinced that her arguments persuaded Senator Mathias to support my nomination in spite of our differences in political philosophy. I had one vote which I had not expected to get.

My biggest problem on the Republican side turned out to be Senator Boschwitz. Even though I had the support of his fellow Republican senator from Minnesota, Dave Durenberger, who also had a background in military intelligence, Boschwitz for some reason appeared opposed to my nomination. I finally was able to schedule what I thought was going to be a private meeting with him. Instead, there was a reporter from *U.S. News & World Report* whom the Senator had invited to join us. I thought, "How could I possibly have a frank discussion with the senator with a reporter in the room taking down everything being said?"

It was not a productive session.

Senator Boschwitz postured in front of the reporter at my expense: "Why should you be named to head ACTION, the volunteer agency, when you have never headed up the United Way campaign in your community as I have in mine?"

What I wanted to say in response was "Well, I am not a multimillionaire like you or the head of a major corporation, and therefore, I haven't been invited to chair a major fund-raising campaign like that." Instead, I responded by recounting some of my volunteer activities, including a stint on the budget committee of our local United Way.

But the meeting went downhill from there. I'd had positive feelings after talking with Mathias, but I came away from my session with Boschwitz more convinced than ever that I would lose his vote.

Since Senator Cranston and Jonathan Steinberg were determined to hold all of the Democrats on the committee together in a party-line vote against my nomination, losing even one Republican vote could prove disastrous.

More trouble was in store when I got a call from Scott Armstrong of the *Washington Post*. He indicated that he was doing a story for his newspaper on my nomination and wanted to get some background information. As I soon learned, getting a call from Armstrong was akin to being contacted by someone from "60 Minutes" who tells you that he wants to do a story on you. The odds are not good that a favorable piece is in the works.

I knew that Armstrong had coauthored a best-seller on the Supreme Court with Bob Woodward entitled *The Brethren*. It had revealed many of the inside details of how the justices conducted their business. I was also aware that Armstrong was considered one of the top investigative journalists at the *Post*.

What I did not know at the time of the call, and subsequently learned from one of my friends in the media, was that Scott Armstrong had close ties to the Institute for Policy Studies (IPS). IPS is a hard left, Washington-based think tank which was very opposed to my replacing Sam Brown at ACTION.

Armstrong and I talked at length over the phone. He wanted to discuss in great detail my service in Vietnam and the Nixon administration, along with my campaign for Congress against Jim Mattox. His lines of inquiry indicated that he was pursuing the idea that I had CIA connections and that I had more assets than I had reported on my financial statements which had been filed in conjunction with my race for Congress and my nomination to be director of ACTION. He asked if he could meet me in the evening at our residence in Chevy Chase, Maryland. I agreed.

As my wife commented after Armstrong left, he must have taken one look at our modest furnishings and concluded that I wasn't hiding assets because he never asked me any more questions on that score. The focus of most of Armstrong's questions that evening was my military service in Vietnam. Without violating my oath to maintain the confidentiality of my "case officer" MOS, I explained to Armstrong what I had done in Vietnam. I told him that I had not been a CIA operative, nor had I worked for the

Phoenix program. But my comments were all for naught. In my opinion, Armstrong already had made up his mind as to what kind of story he wanted to write.

The story that appeared in the *Post* implied that I had worked with the CIA and that my appointment as director of ACTION would lead people to believe that the Peace Corps was engaged in espionage activities. Armstrong conveniently left out of his story the fact that the deputy director position within the Peace Corps had been held in the past by a former military intelligence officer. He didn't let the facts get in the way of his apparent objective of blocking my confirmation.

When the story appeared, I was very upset at the one-sidedness of the article and figured that my nomination was in real jeopardy. I was encouraged however, when an experienced Washington journalist told me not to worry so much. "The story didn't even make page one of the Post. That's a sign the editor didn't think enough of what Armstrong wrote to give it prominent play."

The other thing that began to work in my favor was the outpouring of support from Vietnam veterans. Many were angry that one of their fellow veterans was being penalized for having served in Vietnam. They knew the nomination of Sam Brown, an anti-Vietnam activist, had been approved without opposition during the Carter years. Veterans like Jim Webb (who had had his own differences with Steinberg when Webb worked as a congressional staffer on Veterans Affairs) came to my assistance by contacting friends in the media and on Capitol Hill to object to the treatment I was receiving.

Woody West, then with the *Washington Star,* wrote an editorial supporting my nomination. I myself decided to launch a frontal attack against Jonathan Steinberg who was directing the campaign to smear my reputation.

Thanks to Paul West, a very fair-minded Washington bureau reporter for the *Dallas Times-Herald,* my side of the story was told for the first time in a major newspaper. My question for Jonathan Steinberg was, "You object to what I did in Vietnam. Where were you in the war?" Steinberg had sat out the war in the Washington offices of the Peace Corps. As I expected, he didn't respond to the reporter's attempts to ask him where he had been during the war. He loved to manipulate the political process from behind the scenes, but wasn't willing to undergo public scrutiny as to his own background and political activities.

If I were going down to political defeat at the hands of the New Left crowd, at least I would go down fighting and let people know how the process really worked in Washington. As it turned out, the tide was turning. A number of people on Capitol Hill already resented what they viewed as Steinberg's abuse of his power as a staff assistant. They wanted to see him get his come-uppance. Others objected to my military service being held against me. Senator Hatch, for example, raised this issue directly with Senator John Glenn, a Democratic member of the Foreign Relations Committee, who had had a distinguished military career. Cranston was putting a lot of pressure on Glenn to join the other Democrats on the committee in opposing me. As Senator Hatch told me, Glenn thought it was unfair to attack me for having been a military intelligence officer in Vietnam. I had a chance of winning his vote.

But my opponents had one more card to play. On the day of the hearing, United Press International ran a wire service story alleging that I had been an intelligence case officer in Vietnam and implied that I had CIA connections. The reporter hadn't even bothered to contact me. Her article sounded like something that Jonathan Steinberg might have written. There was something else that bothered me about it. It read as though the reporter had access to my military records, supposedly confidential due to the sensitive nature of my assignment in Vietnam.

I faced a real dilemma. I was about to be sworn in to testify under oath before the Senate Foreign Relations Committee. How should I testify concerning my duties in Vietnam? Upon leaving active duty, I had been told not to discuss or disclose my covert assignment in Vietnam. I had adhered to those guidelines over the years and never talked about my intelligence collection duties except with friends from Vietnam who had the same MOS. How should I respond if asked to discuss those activities at a public hearing in Washington? I didn't want to lie to the committee, but I still believed that I was under orders not to publicly discuss my work in Chau Doc.

By this juncture, everyone involved in the battle over my nomination sensed that it would be approved or rejected based on how I handled the anticipated "cross-examination" from Senator Cranston. After the preliminaries were over, that moment arrived.

Cranston, with Steinberg at his side, bore in on my military duties in Vietnam. I now understood why some reporters referred to the two as "Senator Cranberg." Cranston was reading from a written script which obviously had been prepared for him by Steinberg.

After reading an opening statement criticizing my nomination, Cranston began to ask me questions. After any answer, he would confer with Steinberg before asking his next question. The whole scene would have been humorous had I been an observer rather than the witness in the box. Cranston obviously was looking for a "smoking gun" that he could use to defeat my nomination. That he and Steinberg were so intense in their questioning indicated that they weren't yet confident that they had the votes to defeat me.

Specifically, Cranston demanded that I tell the committee what I did in Vietnam. Trying to stay as general as possible in light of the confidentiality of my work, I indicated that my primary duties in Vietnam were as a province intelligence officer in Chau Duc and as a senior analyst for the Office of Strategic Research and Analysis. This was the truth, but it wasn't what Cranston and Steinberg wanted to hear.

Then Cranston pulled out my military records which he claimed I had authorized him to examine. I sat silently as he made that statement. I never had given him such authorization, but I figured that it would not serve a useful purpose to accuse a U.S. senator of being a liar on his own turf. Cranston proceeded to claim that there was nothing confidential about these records anymore, and that they revealed that I was not telling the truth about my real duties in Vietnam.

My response was that "I would like to be able to see my own records, Senator, in order to be able to fully respond to your questions." We took a break, and Senator Percy's aide on the committee, Chuck Berke, brought me a copy of my personnel file.

I was furious with Percy and made my sentiments known to Berke. "First of all, you have given my records to Cranston and

Steinberg in spite of my specific agreement with the senator that he would not do so. Then, your office doesn't even have the decency to inform me." What I didn't say to Berke (but what I felt at the time) was that Chuck Percy was helping Cranston and Steinberg in their effort to block my confirmation.

Once I had cooled off and had the opportunity to review the records, I felt a little better. My preliminary statement about my duties in Vietnam may have been too general, but it served me in good stead when they tried to portray me as "deceitful" about my Vietnam service. I hadn't lied. I just had left out certain aspects of those duties because of my perceived obligation to keep those matters in confidence. That is what I said when my testimony resumed. Other senators came to my defense along with the *Washington Star* which described the proceedings as taking on the "taint of soldier baiting."

That exchange was the turning point in the confirmation process. Senator Glenn broke ranks with his fellow Democrats and voted to confirm my nomination. All of the Republicans stuck with me except Boschwitz, and I was reported favorably out of committee on a nine to seven vote. Thereafter, I was finally confirmed by the full Senate on a voice vote in May, some three months after my nomination had been sent to Congress.

I had survived the Washington version of the gauntlet and was now at the helm of ACTION.

15

Depoliticizing VISTA

While waiting for the Senate to act on my nomination, I tried to prepare myself for the ACTION job. To aid me in the transition process, a number of experienced conservatives analyzed the major problems I would face at the agency and made recommendations on how to deal with them. Two old friends from College Republican days, John Ryan and Don Thorson, were of immense help in smoothing the way for my transition into the ACTION directorship. The Heritage Foundation had produced an excellent study of the executive branch of government entitled *Mandate for Leadership* that was also very useful to us as we laid plans to change the direction of the agency. Ken Tomlinson and Bill Schulz from *Readers Digest* gave me good advice on how conservatives should deal with the Washington media.

Another conservative friend from the old days who provided me with invaluable counsel and assistance was Neal Freeman, a successful entrepreneur in the television production and syndication business whose ties to the conservative movement dated back to his association with William Buckley, at *National Review*. Neal helped me through the difficult process of selecting capable people for the limited number of political appointments at the agency. He also provided an incisive analysis of the strengths and weaknesses of the ACTION staff and the various agency programs. Neal is a real professional who commanded the respect of those who worked with him at ACTION, and his involvement at this early stage of what became known as "the Pauken administration" gave the career employees at ACTION confidence that changes at the agency would be carefully thought out.

After studying the agency over a period of weeks, Neal's concluding comments were that I had a difficult job ahead of me. He later told me that he thought I faced a hopeless task in changing the direction of ACTION, but didn't want to discourage me.

I wanted to make dramatic changes quickly in a federal agency that had been "radicalized" by my predecessor. To do that, we needed a team of tough-minded conservatives capable of making, and implementing, those difficult decisions necessary to change the direction of ACTION. Putting such a team together became my top priority.

If you want to change the way any federal agency or department operates, you must have the right kind of people in top management positions to help you. Otherwise, bureaucratic inertia and a natural human tendency to protect the status quo will stall any attempts to bring about significant change. Personnel make policy.

As agency director, it was important in the early going that I make wise choices in terms of my key deputies. If I were to be held accountable (as I should be) for the results at ACTION, I wanted to be involved in deciding whom we would hire.

There was a lot of pressure from various Republican congressmen and even the White House personnel office itself to use our agency as a dumping ground for what are called "must hires." That is inside political lingo for party workers and/or people with the right connections who must be given a position somewhere. Under past Republican administrations, ACTION had been used as an employer of last resort for Republicans who needed a job. To his credit, my predecessor Sam Brown had changed the image of

ACTION in that regard by hiring a very smart and dedicated team of New Left activists to run the agency during the Carter years. To undo their agenda and implement our own conservative vision for ACTION, we needed more than just job seekers looking for a place to land.

In one instance I was being pressured by some members of the White House staff as well as prominent Republican leaders to give a woman who owned a fancy spa in California a key post in our agency. I interviewed her and checked her out with some of my contacts who knew her. Not only had she vigorously opposed Reagan's candidacy in the Republican presidential primaries in 1980, she also had a political philosophy at odds with my own—and the President's. She was under consideration for a significant position in the Reagan administration because she was an aggressive job seeker able to assemble an impressive group of supporters who knew her socially or through business connections. Despite a "full-court" lobbying effort on her behalf, I turned her down, only to see her land an even better job in another agency.

Fortunately, I was able to resist having the White House personnel office force appointees on me. Although I made some mistakes in the personnel selection process, they were my mistakes. By and large we were successful in pulling together a talented group of people who believed in the Reagan Revolution. That made a big difference when it came time to make major changes at ACTION.

Once we had our team in place, we established a clearly defined strategy about what we wanted to accomplish during the first Reagan term. In order to avoid any misunderstanding between the political appointees and the career employees at ACTION, we established clear guidelines at the beginning. I never asked a civil servant about his or her politics. Nor did I allow a career employee to be pressured into adopting a particular political line. I did, however, make my goals clear to the ACTION staff and asked for support in making those goals a reality. If some of them did not agree with a particular policy we were considering, they had every right to voice their objections. Once a policy decision had been made, however, everybody was expected to pull together.

Most career civil servants responded favorably to this approach. If what we proposed to do made sense, then most of them were willing to give us a chance to succeed or flop. There were a few exceptions, of course, including certain career bureaucrats who had grown accustomed to running the agency their own way no matter which administration was in office. We Reaganites were viewed as "interlopers." Their attitude was: we were here before you arrived, we will put up with you because we have to, but we will be here long after you are gone.

The fact that administrations come and go while the permanent bureaucracy remains in place is one of the major stumbling blocks to ever getting control over a bloated federal government.

After I was confirmed, an ACTION careerist planned an itinerary for me that would have kept me on the road visiting the various offices of our agency for most of my first few months as director. I guessed that this plan was designed to get me out of the way so that he and his pals could continue to run ACTION on a day-to-day basis.

I declined and decided to stay close to home until our administrative and strategic changes were in place. When the particular group of bureaucrats of whom this fellow was a representative persisted in undercutting our new policy initiatives and kept "hiding the ball" from us on important issues, I decided to shake up the bureaucracy by moving the careerists around a bit. Amazingly, many of these problems disappeared.

One important feature of our personnel policy was to put political appointees in positions of line authority so that Reaganites were overseeing the various divisions of ACTION. If we were going to get the credit or blame for what took place at the agency during the Reagan years, it made sense to put committed conservatives in decision-making positions ranging from the executive officer of the agency, Tim Ryan, to our regional directors such as Paulette Standefer of Dallas.

These steps allowed us to control rather than be controlled by the bureaucracy. Unfortunately, in some other agencies and departments such as the Peace Corps and the Department of Education, administrative and operational authority continued to reside in the hands of the career bureaucracy while political appointees were shuttled off to staff positions where they had no real power. That was no way to change an agency or department in any meaningful way.

One of the most troublesome problems I faced upon my arrival at ACTION was what to do about the tens of millions of tax dollars out of the VISTA budget that Sam Brown was using to fund virtually every kind of leftist organization in the country.

VISTA was a domestic version of the Peace Corps, established as one of LBJ's Great Society programs to help alleviate poverty in America. The so-called volunteers were paid a small stipend plus living expenses to work for a year or more in a poverty-related project. Originally under the Office of Economic Opportunity, VISTA became part of ACTION under a government reorganization plan during the Nixon administration.

Long before I took over at ACTION, VISTA was viewed by many public officials as a highly politicized government program. In a number of communities, VISTA volunteers (who tended to be outsiders) were involved in political organizing activities and took sides in local political disputes. In my hometown of Dallas, for example, VISTA grants during the Carter years went to activist groups ranging from ACORN (Association of Community Organizations for Reform Now) to the Bois d'Arc Patriots.

Sam Brown had turned VISTA into an arm of the New Left political apparatus. He appointed Marge Tabankin, another sixties activist leader, director of VISTA. Tabankin previously had served as the executive director of The Youth Project which, according to Rael Jean Isaac and Erich Isaac in their book *The Coercive Utopians,* operated as a "funnel for tax exempt money to go to radical groups."

Working together, Brown and Tabankin established a VISTA national grants program to channel large sums of money to such leading leftist organizations as ACORN, the Public Interest Research Group (PIRG), the Midwest Academy, and Tom Hayden's Laurel Springs Institute. While the average American has very little familiarity with these groups, political activists on both sides of the battle know how effective these organizations continue to be in advancing the Left's political agenda. For example, the Midwest Academy is a Chicago-based organization, led by former

SDS leader Heather Booth, that trains community organizers using the confrontational techniques developed by the late Saul Alinsky. Once the trainees have been sufficiently radicalized (if they aren't already political radicals by the time they arrive at the institute), they are sent back into their communities or "parachuted" into other cities to help build up the local leftist political network by working for one of the many grassroots organizations that fall under the Left's umbrella.

The Midwest Academy received the largest VISTA grant from Sam Brown in an amount of a half million dollars to train volunteers in community organizing techniques. Here is how the Midwest Academy described a training session for VISTA volunteers in a report to the ACTION office: "The VISTA volunteers' introduction and welcome to the Midwest Academy began with a discussion of what happened politically in the 1960s and what that means in the 1970s. Then, the training session focused in on specific topics such as 'Direct action organizing' and 'How to choose an issue.'"

According to the training manual, the way to pick an issue is to identify a situation in which "we've got an enemy out there." The "enemy" may be a particular company in a city, a local politician, or even the local government itself. First, you identify your issue and your enemy; then, you mobilize people in the community around that issue.

Other topics covered in the Midwest Academy training session for VISTA included: "strategy guidelines," "mapping a campaign," "list your organizations, issues and demands," "write a time line as to how to proceed," "finding and making leaders," and "your constituency."

The VISTA volunteers were given a variety of readings to guide their thinking and actions: *The Tyranny of Structurelessness* by Joe Freeman; *Representative Democracy and SDS; Socialist Feminism and the Making of the English Working Class; The Longest Revolution; Women, Resistance, and Revolution;* and *Making of a Black Revolutionary.* The volunteers also were assigned to read I. F. Stone's *Two Principles* to aid them in the "development of research in relation to organizing." (Stone was one of the few "Old Leftists" looked up to by the sixties radicals.

After the collapse of the Soviet Empire in the late 1980s, a *Human Events* investigative story by Herb Romerstein revealed that Stone had been on the KGB's payroll during much of his journalistic career. This was quite a blow to Stone's admirers who had portrayed him over the years as an iconoclastic defender of individual rights. He died in 1989.)

After the training session that evening, the "students" watched a movie entitled "Burn." The trainees' homework assignment read like a case study out of Harvard Business School with a slight twist:

> You are a researcher for Action to Stop Pollution, an organization in Pittsburgh formed to try to stop U.S. Steel's pollution. You need to show that the company, despite claims of poverty and threats to close up and move, can afford to clean up. This information will help quell community and steelworkers' fears and help enlist support of politicians, church groups, et cetera, plus editorial support from the press. Using the annual report—specifically the balance sheet and income statement, other sections if you have time— and using the readings as a guide, make the best case you can that U.S. Steel can afford pollution control and that they are unlikely to move their plant. Be brief and to the point, but do marshal as much evidence as you can.

As we soon discovered, the ACTION warehouse was loaded with a host of leftist tracts ranging from Saul Alinsky's *Rules for Radicals* to Harry Boyte's *The Backyard Revolution: Understanding the New Citizen Movement*. This literature was being handed out to incoming VISTA volunteers to aid them in their local organizing efforts.

This was how ACTION spent its money prior to Ronald Reagan's victory over Jimmy Carter.

My goal was to eliminate ACTION funding of these activist groups as quickly as possible. I appointed a bright and tough-minded attorney from North Carolina, Jim Burnley, and gave him a mandate to depoliticize VISTA as quickly as possible. I already had met with a number of congressmen and senators who sat on the committees overseeing the ACTION agency, and was pleasantly surprised at their reaction toward my goal of changing the direction of VISTA. Democrats, as well as Republicans, were fed up with many of the abuses that had developed during the Sam Brown years.

Senator Jennings Randolph (D-W. Va.) told me that he was tired of those "outside organizers" being "parachuted" into rural communities in his state with an attitude that they knew what was best for the local residents. Representative Joe Earley (D-Mass.) told me that he wanted an end to the politicization of VISTA that had taken place under the Brown regime.

The only real support in the Congress for the continued federal funding of these activist organizations came from left-wing Democrats like Ted Weiss (New York), Barney Frank (Massachusetts), George Miller (California), and Harold Washington (Illinois). The old style, big city Democrats like Tip O'Neill were no more supportive of Sam Brown's program to "radicalize" VISTA than were the conservative Republicans on our committees. This gave me confidence that we could make major changes in the VISTA program without running the risk of having Congress block our plans.

In an effort to get VISTA under control, I reversed my initial approach of decentralizing authority as much as possible. In one instance, we centralized power over all VISTA grants in our headquarters office. To be approved during those early months, a VISTA grant had to pass muster not only with the state office and the regional office but also with my VISTA Director. Jim Burnley and Mark Levin, a young lawyer from Texas Instruments who had joined my staff, personally reviewed each grant application to make sure that it fell within our new guidelines, which provided that no VISTA funds were to go to politically oriented organizations of the Left or the Right. This approach slowed the approval process down to a virtual crawl for several months, but saved a lot of taxpayer dollars.

Our efforts did not go unnoticed by those most affected by the changes in VISTA. Organizations that had been funded by Sam

Brown and whose grants were not renewed by our administration formed Friends of VISTA to pressure us into abandoning our new policy.

A former VISTA staffer during the Carter years, Mimi Majors, worked full-time as director of Friends of VISTA in an effort to stop us from carrying out the Reagan agenda of defunding the political Left. Since Ms. Majors soon came to the conclusion that she couldn't make any headway with me or Jim Burnley, her best hope for salvaging the VISTA she knew and loved was to stir up opposition to us on Capitol Hill and to generate bad publicity in the media about the "right-wing clique" that had taken over ACTION. She persuaded a writer for newspaper columnist Jack Anderson to report we had a "VISTA hit list" of organizations to be defunded. This was portrayed as a sinister plot on our part to destroy "one of the most important antipoverty programs" of the federal government. We weathered that particular political storm and other attempts by Mimi to stop us. She and the Friends of VISTA served, in effect, as a "government in exile" for the entire four years I spent as director of ACTION.

The Reagan administration had proposed the elimination of VISTA in its first budget submission to Congress. Our legislative director at ACTION was Don Thorson, an experienced and capable Capitol Hill operative. Don and I had started out in politics together as Goldwater conservatives at Georgetown University. He later worked for a number of years as a legislative aide to various conservative congressmen, and offered his assessment of our prospects of getting Congress to go along with the Reagan proposal. As Thorson saw it, Congress might agree to a reduced budget for VISTA, but there was no possibility that the Democratic-controlled House of Representatives would eliminate a Great Society program of the sixties that had become a liberal icon.

In view of the likelihood that VISTA would be continued throughout my tenure at ACTION, I was determined to do what I could to ensure that the monies we appropriated went to deserving organizations. We developed a well-thought-out strategy to make that happen.

My first step was simple enough: apply common sense to the process. I had seen too many examples over the years of federal dollars targeted to help the poor being wasted on projects of dubious worth. In 1968 when I was stationed in El Paso, Texas, at the Defense Language Institute and volunteered at Our Lady's Youth Center in the barrios of South El Paso. The center had an excellent program to help people in the neighborhood get jobs. For a two dollar fee, which paid for the cost of the administrative assistant who ran the program, the applicants would be placed in temporary or permanent positions. It was a low-cost, privately-run and highly-effective jobs program.

But, one day a group of "federales" (as I called them) swooped down from the Office of Economic Opportunity in Washington, D.C., to assess the needs of South El Paso. In the course of their examination of programs already in operation in the barrios, they stumbled upon the jobs initiative at Our Lady's Youth Center. Rather than assist a program that already was operating successfully, the "federales" opened up a competitive jobs program two blocks away which didn't charge any administrative fee. Of course, the cost of running this competitive effort was much higher with staff salaries and overhead required to set up a new program. Costs had been held to a minimum at Our Lady's Youth Center.

It was an example of outsiders with a big pot of federal dollars coming in to make a name for themselves at the expense of local people who had worked hard to develop an effective jobs program for the residents of South El Paso.

There had to be a better way of spending government money to help people in need.

16

Can a Conservative Govern Effectively?

Now I had the opportunity at ACTION to develop an alternative social strategy to the Great Society approach of "throwing" money at problems. I was determined that we not make the same mistakes that I had seen made with federal programs in Bedford-Stuyvesant, Brooklyn, in 1965 and South El Paso in 1968. Our motto was "how to do more with less."

We had three exceedingly bright policy analysts whom I had brought into ACTION to help develop an alternative domestic agenda and steer VISTA away from the community organizing emphasis of my predecessor. Mark Blitz was a brilliant political theorist. He joined us as the director of the Office of Policy and Planning. His two deputies were Connie Horner, a former schoolteacher from D.C., who was an excellent policy analyst, and Richard English, a Goldwater Republican from Texas who had been director of research for George Bush's 1980 presidential campaign.

We decided to concentrate on programs designed to help troubled youth. Our initial emphasis was on drug abuse education and prevention, assistance for runaways, and literacy programs.

The drug issue was one of particular concern to me. As an attorney in private practice in the 1970s, I had represented a number of young people who had gotten in trouble with the law. Most of these kids came from troubled family backgrounds. Some were functional illiterates, although they had attended public schools for ten years or more. Most of the crimes they were accused of committing were drug related—either possession of illegal substances or stealing to feed their drug habit. ACTION had to do something about this explosion of illegal drug use among the young.

As we analyzed the problem of drugs in our society, I was surprised at how ill-informed young people were about the health dangers associated with illegal drug use. Dr. Peter Dupont, one of the leading experts in the field, provided us with statistical data showing that a high percentage of young people in 1981 thought that smoking cigarettes was more dangerous to their health than smoking marijuana. Clearly, students were not being informed about the dangers of marijuana. I had seen too many young people in the seventies who had been harmed by marijuana use. It was far from the "harmless, recreational" drug portrayed by its promoters.

Working with Dr. Carlton Turner, President Reagan's drug policy adviser at the White House, we designed a national campaign to inform young people of the dangers of drug abuse. As we soon discovered, the people who were doing the best job in this field were parents who had seen their own children or friends of their children caught up in the drug culture. A group of volunteer parents had banded together to form the National Federation of Parents for a Drug Free Youth and alert parents and young people to the consequences of illicit drug use. Our agency provided this organization and other grassroots antidrug groups seed money so that they could expand their educational efforts to more communities around the country.

Fortunately, First Lady Nancy Reagan decided to make the drug issue her number one priority. That visibility and public support from the first family on the "war on drugs" really made a difference in the national information campaign to warn young people about the health consequences of illegal drug use.

During the Reagan tenure in the White House, a declining percentage of young people smoked marijuana each year, as evidenced by the results of the annual University of Michigan survey of high school students. Leadership on this issue from the Reagan administration, in conjunction with a volunteer network of businesses and nonprofit associations, really made a difference in diminishing the attractiveness of illegal drugs to young Americans. We at ACTION were pleased to play a major part in that "war."

In addition to our drug abuse education and prevention program, other ACTION initiatives provided assistance to runaway youth shelters such as Covenant House in New York, food banks for the poor, literacy programs, tenant ownership of low income housing, home health care for elderly Americans who preferred to stay in their own homes rather than a nursing home, and programs for latchkey children such as Martha's Table located in one of the roughest areas of Washington, D.C., and Young Volunteers in Action.

Once we determined where we wanted to concentrate our energies, we made sure that funds went to effective groups in those fields. The details of the grant-making process revealed that many of the same old nonprofits that were accustomed to living off federal grants had adjusted their "mission" to fit in with our new initiatives. They were back at ACTION seeking new funding. These were organizations that were good at playing the "grantsmanship" game but didn't do much good with the money once they got it, other than provide salaries for those in charge of the nonprofit agency.

I encouraged our policy staff to search out alternative groups which were not necessarily in the habit of asking the federal government for assistance. This search took a lot of work, but eventually we identified many alternative, nonpolitical organizations deserving of support. We were able to end taxpayer financing of left-wing groups while providing help to some outstanding "social entrepreneurs."

When we discuss the free enterprise system, we use the term entrepreneur to describe individual businessmen who build a successful business through a combination of hard work, the right idea or product, and enough financial resources to make a go of it. In an analogous sense, there is something special about individuals who have a vision and commitment to improve the lot of their fellow human beings in the nonprofit environment. For example, Marva Collins, a public school teacher, took five thousand dollars out of her teacher's pension fund to open her own school to educate supposedly uneducable youth in the inner city of Chicago. Her students and her school both flourished under her remarkable leadership.

She is an excellent example of a "social entrepreneur." These were the types of leaders of nonprofit organizations we were looking to support at ACTION.

For example, we provided funding to the National Center for Neighborhood Enterprise, headed by Bob Woodson, to set up a program of tenant ownership of public housing. With our initial support and as a result of Bob's stellar efforts to convince the Reagan administration of the viability of this idea, tenant ownership programs came into existence in Washington, D.C., and St. Louis, Missouri. Today, this concept is being implemented throughout the country. What Bob Woodson preaches is giving those on the lowest rungs of our economic ladder a stake in this society. In Woodson's view, the Great Society programs designed to assist the underclass in our society perpetuate a politics of dependency. Welfare, food stamps, and public housing simply keep poor folks hitched to the white liberal plantation where they can be more easily manipulated for political advantage.

In our efforts to alter the ACTION grant system, we wanted to be intellectually consistent. I was opposed to the use of taxpayer money to fund political groups of whatever persuasion, and so we refused to use ACTION funds to support conservative political organizations and activities. Leftists on Capitol Hill regularly attacked me for defunding left-wing, community activist groups and complained that I was funding conservative political organizations instead. But it simply wasn't true.

This does not mean that we were socially neutral or indifferent in designing our grant programs. We actively sought out groups with an alternative social vision—groups that were not waiting for the millennium to be rung in through class conflict and social upheaval, but which understood that social improvement should be centered on the improvement of the individual and the community. As a case in point, we provided funds to groups assisting poor, unwed pregnant women who wanted to have the child, rather than an abortion. At the same time, however, we didn't use tax dollars to fund lobbying or legislative activities of antiabortion organizations because that would have crossed the line.

Our alternative agenda worked. One common denominator in all the programs we supported was that our seed money was augmented by a substantial volunteer commitment from the private sector. Another important factor accounting for our success is that the nonprofit groups we funded had strong and broad-based community support. Even the *Washington Post,* a newspaper not known to be sympathetic to the Reagan administration, was forced to admit that we were more effective in carrying out our initiatives than Sam Brown had been.

However, we achieved the greatest results with our Vietnam Veterans Leadership Program (VVLP). As mentioned previously, in the late seventies the popular image of Vietnam veterans varied from psychos to societal victims, something akin to "sick puppies" deserving sympathy. Until VVLP came along, most federal programs encouraged troubled vets to remain preoccupied with the past and what happened in Vietnam.

The overwhelming majority of Vietnam vets resented the public image of veterans as guilt-ridden victims of an unjust war. Like veterans of previous wars, we were proud of our service to our country and were strengthened by it.

VVLP grew out of these sentiments. It was an effort to help Vietnam veterans as a group by countering the derogatory publicity that was so harmful in both an economic and a societal sense. At the same time, the VVLP provided those who really needed help with direct assistance, particularly in the employment arena. The program gave those of us who served in Vietnam the chance to work together one more time.

The program sought to change the public image of Vietnam veterans by stressing that, as in the previous wars fought by Americans, the overwhelming majority of those who returned made a success of their lives. We reinforced this by publicizing the examples of thousands of veterans who had achieved great success in private life. The program also involved successful veterans as volunteers to provide counseling and direct assistance to other veterans who were having problems, whether related to the war or not. We correctly assumed that those who had shared similar experiences and faced many of the same kinds of problems upon returning from Vietnam would be able to help their fellow vets in making it "all the way back."

Moreover, for the first time ever, a program for Vietnam veterans was run from the national to the local level entirely by those who actually served in Vietnam.

A few antiwar activists on Capitol Hill, ranging from Congressman Bob Edgar (D-Penn.) to my old nemesis Jonathan Steinberg from Senator Cranston's staff, tried to block funding for VVLP but failed. The Program enjoyed the personal support of President Reagan and Democratic House Speaker Tip O'Neill. Thanks to my good friend, John Fales, a blinded Vietnam vet who was a first rate public affairs officer at ACTION, Congressman Joe Moakley of South Boston also became an enthusiastic supporter of the VVLP concept.

Joe Moakley was a great friend of veterans, and a lot of residents of South Boston who had served in Vietnam lived and worked in his district. Congressman Moakley was part of Speaker O'Neill's leadership team. He arranged for John Fales and me to have our picture taken with the Speaker. The photo, along with Speaker O'Neill's personal endorsement of VVLP, appeared in the Capitol Hill publication, *Roll Call.* After that, we didn't have any more problems from left-wing Democrats on Capitol Hill intent on scuttling this particular veterans program.

When VVLP was just beginning, one cynic told me that the program wouldn't work: "Pauken, many Vietnam veterans volunteered once before, and look what it got them," he said. "They won't volunteer again." The opposite happened. Veterans from all over the country enthusiastically volunteered for a program which proclaimed that we were proud to have served in Vietnam. Former marines like Jim Webb, author of *Fields of Fire,* who later became secretary of the Navy in the Reagan administration, and

Rick Eilert who wrote *For Self and Country* came aboard early and helped us recruit other outstanding Vietnam vets.

Our Philadelphia chairman was Chuck O'Brien, a successful attorney who had been an army platoon lieutenant in Vietnam. Although he lost a leg in the war, Chuck led a group of handicapped climbers up Mount Rainier and volunteered to help some of his fellow vets ten years after his own injury in the war.

So many outstanding Vietnam veterans banded together to make VVLP a success that it is difficult to single out just a few. A number of these veterans were featured in an ACTION-produced documentary, "When Their Country Called."

Over the past decade, the transformation of public attitudes toward Vietnam veterans has been remarkable. In the late seventies, nearly everything that appeared in print or on screen about Vietnam veterans was negative. Today, this has been reversed: the public attitude toward those who served in Vietnam is overwhelmingly positive. Hollywood has a tougher time trashing our Vietnam soldiers, in spite of films by Oliver Stone.

The Vietnam Veterans Leadership Program contributed greatly to this transformation. I was prouder of what we were able to do together through VVLP than of anything else I accomplished during my four years as director of ACTION.

I'll never forget the day we brought the leaders of VVLP together at the White House for a ceremony. More than a hundred Vietnam vets were in the East Room of the White House as we made our principal supporter, President Ronald Reagan, an "honorary Vietnam veteran." The President couldn't have been more gracious that evening. He told us how much he appreciated that recognition, but that he was there to honor and thank all those in the room and all the other Vietnam veterans, living and dead, who had made great sacrifices in that very difficult war. After the President finished his remarks, you could sense in that room a camaraderie among veterans whose accomplishments had finally been recognized by a president of the United States.

Les Higa, a Japanese-American who chaired our VVLP in Hawaii talked with me later that evening about his feelings as he listened to the president: "When I first came home from Vietnam more than a decade ago, the general reaction to my military service was one of indifference or outright hostility. If anyone would have told me a little more than a decade later that I would be a guest in the White House being thanked by the president of the United States for serving in Vietnam, I would have thought that person crazy."

President Reagan brought the Vietnam veterans home for good.

While we had our successes at ACTION, we also had our share of problems. It was a constant battle to get our agenda implemented, in the face of strong leftist opposition to virtually everything we wanted to do.

When left-wing activists couldn't get Congress to prevent us from changing ACTION, they resorted more and more to "hit pieces" in the media to make us look bad. I guess they really thought they had me when they were able to interest an ABC "20/20" investigative team in doing a story on the relationship between our Vietnam Veterans Leadership Program and the anti-Communist resistance movement in Cambodia.

The media controversy arose as a result of a documentary film our agency made on the resettlement of refugees from Indochina. Hundreds of thousands of people fled South Vietnam, Laos, and Cambodia after the Communist takeover of Indochina. Sometimes, there was a real tension between the new refugees and Americans who didn't have an appreciation of what these people had gone through to escape communism and begin a new life in America. Since ACTION was involved in encouraging volunteers to help in the resettlement of these refugees, we sent a film crew to Thailand to make a documentary film on those who had made their way from Cambodia, Laos, and Vietnam to freedom. The first stop for these refugees from Communism was one of a number of resettlement camps located along the Thai border.

The film, "In Search of Home," was directed by Zack Burkett, a talented documentary filmmaker from Texas who was on our ACTION communications staff. Zack and I had worked together on a number of documentary films in the past. John Rudin wrote the script for the film with help from DeWitt "Pete" Copp, who was the editor of our *Good News Report* at ACTION. Ken Moorefield, a

Vietnam veteran who worked on the VVLP staff, handled the logistics of the trip.

The film was well-received in the refugee community in the United States and was used extensively in training programs for volunteers who worked with Indochinese refugees. Moreover, as a result of the film, some of our Vietnam veterans in Minnesota and elsewhere began to help some of the immigrants adjust to their new home in America. This gave the VVLP an added dimension—American veterans of Vietnam helping Vietnamese veterans of that war.

One day Frank Snepp, a disaffected ex-CIA agent, and Gordon Friedman, a senior producer for "20/20," showed up on my doorstep at ACTION and said they wanted to do a documentary feature on our Vietnam veterans program. They said they were particularly interested in the fact that our veterans were assisting Indochinese refugees. They wanted to know if we had any objection to their interviewing our staff and filming various events surrounding the unveiling of the new documentary. I gave them the go ahead to shoot whatever film they wanted at the agency.

I had no illusions that Gordon Friedman and Frank Snepp were there to do us any favors. Having read Snepp's book on Vietnam, *Decent Interval,* I knew that Snepp was a bitterly disillusioned, onetime member of the American intelligence community with a personal ax to grind. The CIA had tried to prohibit the publication of his book based on the employment contract Snepp had signed with the agency. The agency's lawyers successfully persuaded a court to force Snepp to turn over the profits from his book to the government. Snepp also had a reputation for an excessive reliance on conspiracy theories to explain political and governmental actions. Some of the theories he advanced in his book supported this perception of Snepp as someone who had a tendency to go overboard.

As it turned out, Frank Snepp thought our film was part of a covert CIA operation, utilizing Vietnam veterans to run guns to the anti-Communist resistance in Cambodia. What this latest media controversy was all about was yet another witch hunt to try to connect me and our ACTION programs as the front for a CIA operation.

ABC had brought a film crew to our agency and even sent another one from Washington out to Chicago. Its purpose was to film one of our VVLP meetings.

I guess they expected that our group would be something akin to a gathering of veterans at a Soldiers of Fortune convention. Instead, they saw a lot of veterans who were wearing suits and ties or casual dress. Our guest speaker for the event was Congressman John McCain who later would be elected to the U.S. Senate. John was a much-decorated POW who had displayed incredible courage during his internment in Communist prison cells, and one of our strongest supporters in Congress.

I was speaking to our group of VVLP leaders prior to turning the podium over to McCain. The cameras were rolling throughout my speech and, in fact, the film crew followed me around for much of the weekend, capturing bits and pieces of my conversations with the veterans who were there.

As soon as I finished and McCain came up the podium, the "20/20" film crew began to dismantle their cameras. I would have to have been a fool not to know what was going on. Any producer in his right mind who wanted to do a positive story on VVLP would include footage of a speech to our volunteers by one of the true heroes of the Vietnam War. Yet the folks at ABC had no interest in what he had to say or even in visuals of him talking to our vets.

Since we knew that this was not going to be a friendly piece, I tried to prepare as best I could for an interview with Bob Brown, who would be the reporter on the story. One of us came up with the idea of having our own cameraman in my office filming the interview at the same time that the ABC cameras were there. In this way, if there was unfair editing of my remarks shown on the final version of the "20/20" segment, at least we would have tape of the full interview.

As the ABC crew set up their equipment, they were surprised to see that we had our own cameraman present. My office was packed that day with various ACTION staff members and the ABC production team. Gordon Friedman, the executive producer of this particular segment, showed up personally for the interview. Ironically, Bob Brown had been a reporter for the ABC affiliate in Dallas before joining the network and had always struck me as a fair-minded journalist. Yet, here he was on an apparent mission to show that I was involved in a covert Reagan administration campaign to run weapons to the resistance movement in Cambodia. This entire episode would have been laughable were it not for the fact that Friedman and Snepp were so intent on proving their theory.

For about thirty minutes or so, Brown asked questions designed to elicit information connecting us to a covert operation in Cambodia. After a while, however, he decided to take a break and confer with Friedman.

While the ABC cameraman was taking down his camera to change film, our cameraman continued to film the proceedings. The ABC cameraman became incensed. "You can't do that," he said, as he proceeded to put his hand in front of our camera to prevent us from continuing our filming. Here was ABC doing to us what you so often see on these investigative news programs when someone doesn't want to be filmed.

At some point in the interview, Brown must have concluded that there wasn't anything to Snepp's conspiracy theory. He finally began to ask some straightforward questions about VVLP and about why veterans of the Vietnam war would be involved in an effort to help Indochinese refugees. Had ABC truly wanted to do a story on this subject, it would have made a nice segment for airing. But that wasn't what Snepp and Friedman were looking for, so the story was killed.

Mixed in with our successes at ACTION, and the seemingly never ending battle with liberals in the media who were intent on denigrating our accomplishments, was one major disappointment. We weren't able to integrate the Peace Corps into ACTION and introduce a Reagan-style agenda to that overseas volunteer program.

On the day that I was named to head ACTION, the administration nominated a liberal Republican from Michigan, Loret Ruppe, as director of the Peace Corps. Loret was the wife of Phil Ruppe, a former Republican congressman turned Washington lobbyist. She had been active in George Bush's presidential primary campaign in 1980. Loret made it clear from the outset that she wasn't interested in seeing the Peace Corps remain a part of ACTION.

Although the Reagan transition team had recommended that the Peace Corps be folded into ACTION and that the director of that agency oversee both foreign and domestic volunteer programs, the Ruppe appointment effectively undercut that policy recommendation. On her own and in opposition to administration policy, Loret privately sided with the Peace Corps constituency and liberal forces on Capitol Hill in supporting proposed legislation to turn the Peace Corps into an independent agency, again in the event that I was confirmed as ACTION director. (The Peace Corps had been established as an independent agency by JFK, but Richard Nixon had combined it with domestic volunteer programs during his administration and called the new agency ACTION.)

Once I was confirmed, the liberals launched a major lobbying campaign in Congress to take away my jurisdiction over the Peace Corps. Leading the fight against us was "my old friend" from Senator Cranston's staff, Jonathan Steinberg. When Sam Brown had headed the agency, Cranston had opposed the separation of Peace Corps from ACTION. With me in charge, the senator and his top aide took a decidedly different stance. Only this time they were more successful than in blocking my nomination to head ACTION.

I really was in a no-win situation. Steinberg and his friends had planted stories in the foreign press claiming that Peace Corps volunteers would be killed if a former "intelligence agent" like me had any involvement whatsoever with the Peace Corps. It was meaningless to Steinberg that other former military intelligence personnel had served in the Peace Corps. Putting out misinformation overseas suggesting that my appointment was some kind of a CIA plot to take over the Peace Corps could encourage extremist groups in Third World countries to harm Peace Corps volunteers. I decided to separate myself entirely from any aspect of my duties that might involve decisions affecting the Peace Corps. When Steinberg and others later fought to take the Peace Corps out of ACTION, we didn't even bother to mount an opposition campaign since that battle had been effectively lost during the confirmation process.

You can't win them all.

Yet, the question still remains: Can a conservative govern effectively? The way Washington works puts conservatives at a decided disadvantage. If you are a conventional liberal or pragmatist who does not disturb the "business as usual" attitude in Washington, you get far better treatment in the media and on Capitol Hill as an agency or department head than if you are a conservative holding a similar position.

As I see it, the rules aren't going to change in the foreseeable future; if you don't like the way the game is played, you can pick up your football and go home. Conservatives simply have to understand that, while they may not be on a level playing field in Washington, they have to persist even when the rules are weighted against them. Understanding these political facts of life will go a long way toward helping conservatives learn how to govern effectively.

I am convinced that conservatives can change the direction of our government. It can be difficult at times, and frustrating to no end. Yet a team of conservatives, working together with a clear and consistent agenda, can bring about dramatic change in an agency or department. Within a four-year period at ACTION, our Reagan team managed to cut the staff from more than a thousand to five hundred, reduce the budget by 25 percent (from $160 million to $120 million), and eliminate funding of leftist political organizations. Simultaneously, we developed an alternative social policy to the Great Society approach of helping the poor which accomplished more with less money.

When someone says change is too difficult, the bureaucracy is too entrenched, or Congress won't cooperate, my response is: You are doing something wrong. If one has the substantive ability to handle the job, is sophisticated politically, and (most important of all) has the courage of one's convictions, it is possible to succeed—even in Washington. Perhaps, in the next conservative administration, we will have more opportunities to prove it.

17

Battling the New Left

One means by which radical organizations have managed to stay afloat is through their well-developed talent for getting financial support for their activities from government agencies, foundations, and church groups. When I was the director of ACTION, I turned off the spigot, only to discover that a poverty arm of my own church was heavily supporting the same activist groups I was fighting to defund.

My first inkling of what was going on came when I picked up the newspaper one day and read that a Catholic priest named Marvin Mottet, who headed the Campaign for Human Development (CHD), had denounced the Reagan administration for its cuts in the VISTA program.

I knew the reductions we were making were directed at organizations which never should have received taxpayer funding in the first place. So I decided to take a look at the funding pattern of CHD which referred to itself as a poverty-fighting organization. Imagine my surprise as a Catholic to discover that millions of dollars raised from Catholic parishioners (most of whom, I suspect, were unaware as to where their contributions were going) were being sent to many of the same left-wing groups I had recently defunded at ACTION.

Mottet himself was a former political organizer for ACORN, one of the most confrontational groups on the left. Originally founded as the National Welfare Rights Organization by Wade Rathke, a sixties radical, the group had changed its name to ACORN to attract broader support, but it continued to emphasize the tactics of intimidation favored by Saul Alinsky when it took on various "targets."

The late Saul Alinsky wrote the leftist organizing bible, *Rules for Radicals*. In the forward to the book, Alinsky offered: "an over-the-shoulder acknowledgment to the very first radical...who rebelled against the establishment and did it so effectively that he at least won his own kingdom—Lucifer."

Over the years, many young nuns and priests had fallen under the spell of Saul Alinsky, who based his community organizing operation in Chicago. Alinsky had decided early on in his career that he had to change the attitudes of the Catholic church in the United States which traditionally had been viewed as a conser-vative, anti-Communist religious institution. His objective was to use his young "recruits" from the religious ranks as a wedge inside the institution of the church in order to change it. As the Alinsky-trained recruits grew older and gained more power within the Church infrastructure, the Catholic Church in America began to show the effects.

The radicalization of elements of the Catholic clergy turned out to be one of Saul Alinsky's most significant accomplishments. His decades of hard work paid off as the religious who shared Alinsky's radical brand of politics moved into key positions of influence within the bureaucracy of various religious orders, Catholic dioceses, and even the United States Catholic Conference itself (the national organization of the American bishops).

In addition to the hundreds of thousands of dollars it received from Sam Brown at ACTION, ACORN was given over a million dollars in grant money from the Catholic-funded Campaign for Human Development over a ten-year period. In fact, its largest grants during the time Mottet ran CHD went to "community-organizing projects of the Alinsky school: the largest single recipient has been the Industrial Areas Foundation, founded by Alinsky."

Since its founding in 1972, the Campaign for Human Development has been under the direction and firm control of Alinsky-style activists who have dispensed well over $100 million to kindred organizations across the country. That's quite a nest egg to help keep organizations viable in a less than favorable political environment. The success of the New Left in holding its forces together during the Reagan era is testimony to its ability to do "whatever works."

As Pope John Paul II appoints more American bishops whose beliefs mirror his own about the role of the Catholic Church in the world, there is a strong likelihood that at some point in the not too distant future CHD will end its funding of groups with a secular, political agenda. This will come as a major blow to the American Left.

In addition to my running battle with remnants of the New Left over VISTA funding, my last major assignment as a Reagan official led to a political dispute with an Alinsky-style organization in the Rio Grande Valley.

In 1967, prior to starting my course in Vietnamese at the Defense Language Institute in El Paso, I represented then-Congressman George Bush at a major U.S.-Mexico meeting known as the Chamizal Conference. President Johnson was handing Mexico some disputed border property and holding a conference at the same time to address the concerns of Mexican-American leaders on public policy issues. The Johnson administration saw the gathering as an opportunity to court the Hispanic political leadership.

I had first met George Bush at his Houston home in 1965 when I was campaigning for national chairman of the College Republicans. Bush was gracious enough to help me in that effort. I already had been an enthusiastic supporter of his candidacy in 1964 when he lost a race for the U.S. Senate to Ralph Yarborough. George Bush struck me as a thoughtful conservative who had the potential to go all the way to the White House. I suspect that I became one of the first Bush-for-President boosters back in the 1960s.

I had stayed in touch with him after his election to Congress in 1966. When I informed him that I had been assigned to language school in El Paso, he asked me if I could attend the Chamizal Conference on his behalf and prepare a report for him on the concerns of the Mexican-American leadership in attendance. At this particular time in Texas politics, the general assumption was that Mexican-Americans were wedded to the Democratic party, but Bush was savvy enough to sense that the Republican party needed to pay more attention to the views and attitudes of these Americans.

It was a fascinating conference for a young man like me who was unfamiliar with how disenchanted many Mexican-American leaders had become with the Democratic party. A major dispute broke out at the conference when the presidential motorcade, including President Johnson, the president of Mexico, and Texas Governor John Connolly, conveniently left Senator Ralph Yarborough (who was feuding with Governor Connolly at the time) in a car at the rear of the parade. At the time, conservative Democrats led by Connolly and liberal Democrats led by Yarborough were battling for control of the Texas Democratic Party. Mexican-Americans had tended to side with the Yarborough faction, and many in attendance at Chamizal were angry over this slight of their leader.

Throughout the conference proceedings and in informal discussions, many of the Mexican-American leaders made it plain that they were tired of being taken for granted. What the Johnson political camp had hoped would become a political love-fest turned into a forum for Mexican-American leaders to express their real views and concerns.

In a report prepared for Bush, I pointed out that the values articulated by most of the leaders were very "simpatico" to the basic principles of the Republican party. It appeared to me that it would be foolish to ignore a large number of citizens whose basic belief system was so similar to our own. The importance of family, neighborhood, a sense of community, religion, patriotism, and a strong work ethic, all were values emphasized by many of the Hispanic leaders in attendance. In particular, a number of the speakers made note of the high percentage of Mexican-Americans who had volunteered for military service and been honored for their valor in combat.

In addition to making some specific recommendations in regard to issues that had been addressed at the conference, I expressed to George Bush my perspective that he and other Republican political leaders should take an active role in bringing Mexican-Americans into the party. He was enthusiastic about the concept of reaching out to people who previously had been ignored by the national Republican Party and followed up on many of my recommendations.

Some of those present at Chamizal later attempted to establish an independent Hispanic party known as La Raza Unida, an effort at separatist politics which ultimately failed. Others, encouraged by party leaders like George Bush and John Tower, joined the Republican Party. Thereafter, the Republicans would make substantial inroads into the Hispanic community which, until Chamizal, had been solidly in the Democratic camp.

In 1970, while on the Nixon staff with John Dean, I was asked to prepare a background paper on an administration initiative associated with the cabinet committee on Spanish-speaking affairs. I already had concluded that Mexican-Americans were not necessarily wedded to the Democratic party. Now, I was in a position to encourage the administration, and the Republican party, to do more to attract Hispanics to our cause. I argued in the position paper that was going to the President that as Republicans we should show how similar fundamental beliefs of the Hispanic community and the Republican party were. I urged that we welcome to our ranks a group of Americans whose commitment to the values of family, neighborhood, work, patriotism, and religion made them natural allies.

In the end, the administration undertook a major initiative on that front through the cabinet committee on Spanish-speaking affairs. No longer were the Democrats automatically able to count on the vote of Mexican-Americans in the Southwest.

In 1984 the border region of south Texas known as the Valley had been dealt a double economic whammy. The peso devaluation in Mexico had decimated retail businesses along the border that were heavily dependent on business from Mexican nationals. With the peso losing much of its value against the dollar, many of these people no longer could afford to shop in the United States. In addition, a devastating freeze had put a lot of farm workers on the unemployment lines. The Valley already had more than its share of social and economic problems without these added disasters clobbering the region. Unfortunately, the problems were exacerbated by a slow response from the federal machinery in charge of providing disaster relief.

With all these problems facing the people in the Valley, it didn't take long for a local affiliate of the Industrial Areas Foundation (IAF), an Alinsky-created umbrella organization, to get into the act. A group calling itself Valley Interfaith announced that it intended to act as the representative of the people in the Valley in establishing and overseeing a massive public works program which would be funded by the federal government. Demands were being made on the Reagan administration for an immediate response to Interfaith's public works proposal.

In a widely publicized address before the National Press Club in Washington, D.C., the Democratic governor of Texas, Mark White, had fueled the political fires by denouncing the administration's lack of response to the Valley's problems.

I was dispatched by the White House to the Rio Grande Valley to assess the overall situation and to figure out a way to speed up the federal response to the economic disaster. I knew I was walking into a political hornets' nest and had no illusions that this would be an easy assignment. As I saw it, the most difficult part of my assignment would be to figure out how to deal with this Alinsky-style group which was claiming to represent the majority of people in the Rio Grande Valley. The leaders of the Valley Interfaith organization saw the problems as an opportunity to gain a political foothold along the Texas-Mexico border.

Valley Interfaith was a classic example of a New Left organization all dressed up for the eighties. Its founder was Ernesto Cortes, a sixties activist, who was acknowledged to be the most successful Alinsky-style organizer in the Southwest. Cortes had been part of a contingent of former radicals who met with Sam Brown and Marge Tabankin during the early days of the Carter administration to chart a new direction for VISTA. During the seventies, Cortes had organized a grassroots organization in San Antonio known as C.O.P.S. At one point it became the most powerful political organization in that city. With the success of C.O.P.S. behind him, Cortes decided to establish a network of similar local organizations throughout the state with particular emphasis on border communities with a substantial Mexican-American population.

Cortes enjoyed the active support of the Catholic archbishop of San Antonio and Catholic bishops in El Paso and Brownsville. All of Saul Alinsky's hard work in recruiting religious support from within the Catholic church was now paying off as the dioceses threw their weight behind Cortes's organizational efforts. The Alinsky organizers even had their own training institute in San Antonio to educate the clergy and civilians on "social justice" issues. Cortes was one of the instructors at the Mexican-American Cultural Center (MACC) which was directed at that time by Fr. Virgil Elizando, another Alinsky disciple. The curriculum at MACC emphasized the principles of "liberation theology" and the development of "base communities" in the barrios and depressed neighborhoods. Carried to its logical extreme, liberation theology is an attempt to blend the principles of Christianity and Marxism into a common philosophy. Critics of MACC have noted that the version of liberation theology being taught at that institute seemed very similar to that being advocated by the so-called Christian Marxists—a viewpoint rejected by Pope John Paul II and his leading theological adviser Cardinal Ratzinger as incompatible with Christian principles.

The base communities were the organizational vehicle through which the liberation theologians would try to create a society based on the principles of "Christian Marxism." The model for this "new society" was the Sandinista regime in Nicaragua which used base communities to establish a so-called popular church independent of the Catholic hierarchy.

Ernie Cortes taught a course on base communities at MACC. That gave him access to groups of students, clergy, and lay leaders who were potential community organizers for his various IAF affiliates in the Southwest. This was important to Cortes who was trying to build on his initial success with C.O.P.S. in San

Antonio by expanding his political network into El Paso and the Rio Grande Valley.

As had been the case in San Antonio, Cortes was able to elicit the enthusiastic backing of the local Catholic bishop, Bishop Pena, for his project. Local Catholic churches in El Paso were "encouraged" to join as dues-paying members of this new community-based organization called E.P.I.S.O. What was represented to be an interfaith alliance of churches and local leaders to improve the conditions of the people in the poorer, predominantly Hispanic neighborhoods in El Paso was in reality the nucleus of what Cortes and his associates hoped would be the most influential political force in this Texas border city.

While E.P.I.S.O. enjoyed some initial success, there was tremendous opposition from local Catholics who resented their churches and funds being used to support a secular, political movement. Consequently, IAF organizers did not achieve the degree of influence in El Paso that they had enjoyed in San Antonio.

It was then that Cortes and his cohorts launched Valley Interfaith. Jim Drake, a Protestant minister who had been one of Cesar Chavez's closest advisers in California, was brought into the Valley to run the operation. Again, Cortes was able to get backing from the local Catholic bishop.

The centerpiece of Valley Interfaith's program was a plan demanding that the Reagan administration spend in excess of $70 million for temporary public service jobs for Valley residents and migrant farm workers thrown out of work because of the winter freeze and subsequent damage to the crops. Since the local bishop had thrown his full weight behind the Valley Interfaith agenda, the message went out to all of the Catholic parishes in the diocese that priests and parishioners were expected to support this "social justice" initiative. While I suspect that most of the pastors were not all that familiar with the political agenda of this organization, they were loyal priests and did what they were asked to do by their local bishop. This support from the bishop enabled Cortes and Drake to recruit a leadership core and a large number of followers.

Before long, Valley Interfaith took on the appearance of a powerful organization with thousands of supporters. As Saul Alinsky repeatedly pointed out to his followers, the "perception of power" is the first step in convincing people that you have real power. Valley Interfaith was on its way to achieving its objective as *the* political power broker in south Texas.

Cortes and Drake stepped up their efforts on a variety of fronts. Interfaith organizers put pressure on local public officials to sign petitions of support for its massive public works proposal. Simultaneously, IAF leaders carefully cultivated the press to publicize its activities in the Valley. The media throughout Texas and even nationally began running stories which, for all practical purposes, could have been written by the IAF organizers themselves. Almost uniformly, the stories recounted the plight of the Rio Grande Valley whose condition was akin to that of a "Third World" region and presented Valley Interfaith as the only viable force in that region trying to do anything about these serious problems.

There was one other "cute" feature associated with the demands that the Reagan administration fund a massive public works program. The proposed temporary jobs under the Interfaith proposal would run out in September 1984, conveniently in advance of the November presidential election. Ernie Cortes and Jim Drake had cooked up a clever scheme; one of those heads I win, tails you lose, propositions. If Valley Interfaith got all or part of the money it was demanding from the federal government, it would be a major victory for this relatively new organization. If the Reagan administration refused to fund the jobs proposal, Interfaith activists could attack the president for his insensitivity to the plight of the people in the Valley.

I did not have an easy task ahead of me.

Having dealt with New Left activists since the sixties, I had probably accumulated as much institutional knowledge of their political modus operandi as anyone. My experience over the years in dealing with fronts was that there was always a hidden agenda beneath their publicly proclaimed objective of "righting a wrong."

What I didn't know in this case, prior to my first trip to the Valley, was how much real support Valley Interfaith had among the populace at large and among the local elected officials. Did this organization have only an appearance of power?

The first thing that I did when I arrived in the Rio Grande Valley was to meet privately with local community leaders and elected officials to get their assessment of the overall situation and their off-the-record feelings about Valley Interfaith. None of the local leaders I met with cared for the group's confrontational tactics. They particularly resented the intimidation of local elected officials in so-called accountability sessions. These were meetings designed to force the local politicians to go along with Valley Interfaith's agenda for their own political good. The technique of intimidating local politicians into signing petitions in support of the Interfaith proposal worked in the short term, but created hard feelings on the part of the local politicians, almost all of whom were Democrats.

In private, many of these officials expressed anger over being embarrassed and humiliated in carefully stage-managed public meetings run by IAF organizers. A number of local politicians were outraged over what they perceived to be a group of outsiders trying to come in and take over the Valley for their own purposes. It didn't take many private meetings with local leaders for me to realize that Valley Interfaith did not have the community support it claimed.

While Cortes and Drake were doing all they could to use the Valley disaster to build a political machine, Texas Democratic Governor Mark White was taking advantage of the situation for his own reasons, castigating the Reagan administration for its slow response to the economic disaster. Yet, much of the fault rested with the state bureaucracy in Austin. The governor's own departments had been slow in processing designated federal funds which first had to go through the state government prior to being sent to the Valley.

The situation I faced was complicated. The disaster was real—the people in the Rio Grande Valley were hurting. The bureaucracy had been slow to respond. Mark White and Valley Interfaith leaders were taking rhetorical potshots at the Reagan administration. I had to move quickly. To avoid a two-front political war, I simply announced at a press conference that henceforth state and federal officials would work together in a cooperative fashion, rather than at cross-purposes, in responding to the needs of those in the Valley. Further, to ensure that the various governmental officials cooperated with one another, I indicated that I would meet personally with the governor to work out the details.

Meanwhile, I already had been in touch with one of the governor's top aides. I told him that we could either work together to get something accomplished, or we could spend our efforts on blaming each other for the slow bureaucratic reaction to the problems in the Valley. I also pointed out to him that the state government had not done a very good job in expediting assistance to the people in south Texas. So, if the governor wanted to continue to play politics with the situation in the Valley, we knew how to play, too.

Reluctantly, Governor White agreed to meet with me. He didn't have a smile on his face or a warm greeting as I was ushered into his office in the state capitol building, and was obviously less than enthusiastic about seeing me. I went ahead anyway with an overview of our plans for responding to the crisis in the Valley. I explained how we looked forward to working with his staff in a cooperative manner to help deal with this matter of common concern to President Reagan and himself.

Governor White didn't have much to say in response, and after we were finished, one of his assistants guided me out the back door. I assumed that the reason for sending me out the back way was to avoid alerting the capitol press corps to our meeting. It didn't make any difference to me since I had no intention of talking with the press afterwards. I had accomplished my purpose. Thereafter, the political attacks against the president from Governor White ceased and I was able to focus on developing a plan of action.

Back in Harlingen, Texas, I began to see some improvement in the federal response to the economic disaster. We established a list of priorities, and I set up a Valley ACTION Committee composed of local community leaders to advise me. Tom Champion, a Mexican-American leader from the Brownsville area, who was the chairman of the Valley Chamber of Commerce, agreed to head that committee.

When a reporter asked me what role Valley Interfaith would play in this process, I responded that I would be happy to meet with their organization as with any other group which requested a meeting. The journalist pressed me to more fully define their involvement in our program. I answered that, as far as I understood, no one had elected the Interfaith officials to speak for the people in the Valley. Consequently, I would rely more on the locally elected officials and longtime community leaders for advice on how we should respond to this crisis.

Jim Drake blew up over my comments. In effect I had announced for the first time publicly that Valley Interfaith no longer was setting the agenda for the governmental assistance plan for south Texas. With local media in tow, Drake showed up at the Sheraton Hotel in Harlingen where we were holding meetings with various groups to discuss our Valley initiative.

In their typical confrontational style, the IAF crew stormed into the conference room at the hotel which was serving as the unofficial center of our operations. Drake had brought about fifteen or twenty representatives of Interfaith along, but he did most of the talking. He demanded that I meet with them to discuss their public jobs proposal for the Valley. I replied that I already had a series of meetings scheduled for the afternoon, but that I could meet with them that evening. Drake and one older Anglo directed a number of disparaging comments toward me in an attempt to let me know that I had better cooperate with their organization's agenda. The obvious purpose of these implicit threats was to pressure me into accepting Valley Interfaith into the decision-making process before the development and implementation of any plan of action for Valley relief.

I tried to deflect personal attacks in order to avoid a confrontation at the time and hold off discussing our differences until later that evening. I noticed that there was one young Hispanic priest in the group who didn't seem to belong with Drake and some of the others. He had a look on his face that said he was trying to sort out for himself what the truth was with respect to our dispute. I was glad to see that he didn't return with Drake and the others that evening.

I knew ahead of time how the IAF crowd played the game. By my not acceding to their demands, I would be made to pay a personal price for my "lack of cooperation." Sure enough, Valley Interfaith leaders denounced me at a hastily called press conference, held at a prominent religious shrine. Ernie Cortes got on the horn to his liberal friends in the Texas media to stir up anti-Pauken articles and editorials about my work.

One of the most scathing personal attacks was written by Molly Ivins, then the resident left-wing columnist for the *Dallas Times-Herald*. She pilfered parts of an attack previously written by Colman McCarthy in the *Washington Post* who was upset over our decision to stop using VISTA to fund leftist organizations. Molly added her own two cents worth about my confrontation with her buddy Ernie Cortes in the Valley. Although it is never pleasant to find yourself denounced in the press (even considering the source), I was amused by the quote from Cortes in the Ivins hit piece: "Pauken has a lower political intelligence than Jim Watt."

One more public encounter remained. It was apparent that this was going to be a very heated session. I was glad that a few of my friends and associates would be with me.

Fortunately, one of those in attendance was H. "Pulse" Martinez, a small businessman from San Antonio and strong supporter of President Reagan. Pulse had taken time off from his business to assist me in putting together an effective plan for Valley relief. The more Pulse and I worked together, the more impressed I was with his insights into the best way of handling certain problems. There is a word in Spanish, *compadre,* which means a friend so close that you would trust him to be the godfather of your children. Compadre is the right word to describe my feelings for Pulse Martinez after we went through some very difficult battles together in south Texas.

Most public officials who have had to endure one or more of these so-called accountability sessions realize how much prior planning goes into structuring these meetings in order to achieve the desired results. In fact, the Midwest Academy even provides its students with a suggested script as to how to manipulate meetings to put their opponent on the defensive. The purpose of this tactic is to so intimidate and/or anger their opponent that he either capitulates to the demands of the group or becomes so angry at the criticism directed at him that he overreacts by saying or doing something which he later will regret. By overreacting, the "target" suddenly finds that his "mistake" is featured prominently in local media coverage of the dispute. The script laid out for these sessions attempts to show the Alinsky-trained organizers how to win the confrontation, no matter how the various "targets" react to the demands made of them.

Jim Drake had done his job well. He had picked local leaders who either had a preexisting openness to the type of class warfare advocated by IAF or who had been radicalized as a result of the IAF training process. These community organizers had been fully indoctrinated in the Alinsky principles of class warfare.

The local media was out in full force that evening. One Valley television station had sent over its crew an hour in advance to make sure that their cameraman was properly positioned to film the session from beginning to end. The press anticipated an explosion of some sort, and, of course, that would make for great visuals on the ten o'clock news as would front page stories with accompanying photos in the Valley newspapers the next day. It was one of those "media events" that I had to get through without any major blunders in order to move on to the real business: implementing our Valley ACTION plan.

When a group of some thirty to forty Interfaith activists crowded into the conference room that evening, it quickly became apparent to me that Drake's forces were in a highly agitated state. I had never been in any political setting, even during the height of the Vietnam war debates on unfriendly college campuses, where the level of hostility was as intense as it was in that room. I don't use the word hate lightly, but there is no other appropriate word to describe the expressions on the faces of some of that group as they vented their anger at me. To this group, I was known as *el alarçon,* which is Spanish for the scorpion.

Some of those who were part of the Interfaith crowd were sincere and decent people who did not fit the above description. I could see in their faces that they were not consumed with rage, but simply wanted answers to some questions about Valley problems or were there at the request of their pastors. But these people were not part of the leadership corps of the organization.

Jim Drake positioned his forces so that the primary spokesperson for the group would be a young Hispanic woman seated directly across the table from me. The symbolism was obvious.

If I could be provoked into overreacting at some stage of the proceedings, how would that display of temper look on the ten o'clock news? You could almost visualize the scene: white, Anglo bureaucrat from Washington, D.C., insults local Hispanic woman involved in program to help the needy. I didn't intend to take the bait.

During the course of what Interfaith viewed as my accountability session, the Hispanic spokeswoman accused me of being a Washington outsider who didn't know anything about south Texas. I pointed out in response that I was a native south Texan, having been born in Victoria, Texas. That hardly made me an outsider. While this exchange was going on, other charges were being made surreptitiously. As Pulse Martinez told me after the meeting, one member of Interfaith in the back of the room began whispering in Spanish that I must be anti-Catholic. Pulse Martinez replied in Spanish that I was a Catholic. Later in the evening, the next rumor to make the rounds was that I was anti-Mexican. Again, Pulse responded in Spanish, since my wife is Mexican-American, it was unlikely for me to have this bias. So, the Interfaith organizers were left with Drake's description of me as *el alarçon.*

Meanwhile, the acrimonious exchange continued with Interfaith organizers doing most of the talking. Borrowing a page right out of their Midwest Academy script, one of the activists accused me of McCarthyism. My response to that charge was that they were the people engaged in making unwarranted personal attacks that evening, which is what I thought was the dictionary's definition of McCarthyism. I added that, as far as I was concerned, their tactics of resorting to character assassination in order to run over anyone who got in their way amounted to a "new McCarthyism" of the Left.

The tenor of the meeting went downhill from there. Jim Drake sat in the back of the room orchestrating the performance of his cast like a puppeteer, according to one observer. But their attempts to provoke me to lose my temper didn't work. Nor had my responses to their demands and personal attacks been as they had anticipated. It must have thrown Drake and his top leaders off guard. After a while, the confrontation began to wind down and peter out. I had survived an IAF accountability session and had emerged relatively unscathed. Now that Valley Interfaith had fired its "big guns" at me without notable success, I felt confident that we could move on to more constructive endeavors.

I was in good spirits later that evening as I had dinner with Pulse Martinez in Mexico, feeling that we finally were about to put the Valley Interfaith controversy behind us. My sense was that an increasing number of community leaders in the Rio Grande Valley were fed up with the abrasive rhetoric and tactics of the Valley Interfaith crowd. If we put those leaders together with those who already were working with us, we would have a formidable team.

Pulse Martinez was much more astute than I that evening in explaining why my problems with Valley Interfaith were far from over. Pulse warned me, "Now that they see that they can't get you to deal with them, and, since they haven't been able to provoke you into doing or saying something stupid that would get you into trouble, Cortes and Drake will try to get rid of you in another way." Pulse's guess was that Valley Interfaith would try to go around me and attempt to deal with others in the administration who might be more accommodating.

While I listened to what my friend had to say, I thought he was mistaken. The political winds were shifting in our favor. We were making substantial headway in enlisting broad-based community support for our program while extricating the administration from a political trap that had been set for it by an organization diametrically opposed to the Reagan agenda.

Well, Pulse Martinez was right. Within a matter of days, Jim Cicconi (one of Jim Baker's top staff aides) tracked me down in Austin to chew me out for screwing everything up in the Valley, thus creating serious problems for the Reagan administration. Even though I knew immediately that Cicconi was calling me at the behest of James Baker, I was flabbergasted at his comments and was not particularly deferential in responding. I told Cicconi that, as far as I was concerned, sitting in a soft chair in Washington, D.C., didn't give him the best vantage point from which to determine what was going on in the Valley.

Heading back to Washington, I sensed that something was up. Obviously, Baker had decided that I had become a political liability. My assessment was confirmed when a well-placed friend within the administration pulled me aside and warned me that I was about to be thrown overboard. The White House was planning to pull me out of the Valley and replace me with someone more "moderate" in approach.

As I later learned, the leaders behind the Interfaith organization had utilized some of their contacts within the Republican hierarchy to get the message to the "right people" that they would work with just about anybody else in the administration on Valley issues if it just got rid of Pauken.

Ernie Cortes had come up with a brilliant stratagem. Previously, the Alinsky gang had managed to get their liberal allies in the media, like Molly Ivins, to crank out negative articles on me in various Texas dailies. These, they just sent along to the right people with the ability to influence administration policy. The hoped for result was that I would be pulled out of the Valley. Cortes was borrowing a page from the "liberal playbook." For decades liberals have used Establishment-minded publications, like the *Washington Post* and the *New York Times,* to run stories designed to undercut the policy initiatives of determined conservative policy makers.

One dirty little secret about Washington politics is that, if you play the game by acquiescing to the status quo, i.e., liberal dominance of the policy-making process, then the allies of the liberals in the media will repay the favor by portraying you in a neutral or even positive fashion. Jim Baker knew how to play this game about as well as any Republican insider in Washington.

Ironically, while all of this behind the scenes maneuvering was going on within the administration, the preponderance of the media coverage in the Rio Grande Valley was turning against Valley Interfaith as local reporters began to focus more closely on the political agenda of Ernie Cortes and Jim Drake. I knew if I could buy a little time before the Baker group replaced me with one of their own, we could get the situation turned around in the Valley in terms of popular support for our plan of action.

Prominent Reagan conservatives such as Lyn Nofziger, Sen. Paul Laxalt, and Bill Clark came to my defense. They knew instinctively that you couldn't do business with a hard-left, activist group like Interfaith. Their backing prevented the Baker faction from removing me as the administration's liaison to the Rio Grande Valley.

Shortly thereafter, our efforts began to show results. Working closely with Tom Champion, chairman of our Valley ACTION Committee, we began to identify and remove federal impediments to disaster assistance to the Valley.

John Fales of our ACTION staff worked closely with a group of veterans in south Texas to develop a plan to improve job and educational opportunities for the many Vietnam-era veterans in that region. Another ACTION staffer, G. G. Garcia, who had been a city manager previously in the Valley, worked with local officials to make sure that the federal bureaucracy was responsive to their concerns.

A Democratic friend of mine, Jim McFadden, who formerly had been commissioner of labor for New York City and who had close ties to the American labor movement, helped to develop a manpower training project to upgrade the skills of Valley workers. Many others worked closely with us on a variety of projects to develop public-private partnerships that would have a rippling effect on the Valley economy. We weren't interested in short term fixes like the Interfaith solution of a four month public works program.

Valley residents began to see that the Reagan administration was truly concerned with their plight. It even got to the point to where I was accused at a Congressional hearing chaired by Democratic Congressman Barney Frank of Massachusetts of diverting too many federal dollars from other regions and into south Texas.

Of course Valley Interfaith leaders continued to attack me personally throughout the summer of 1984. Yet, though they were able to get their left-wing political allies from Texas—such as Democratic senatorial candidate Lloyd Doggett and Agricultural Commissioner Jim Hightower—to join in the "Pauken bashing," people in the Valley didn't pay much attention anymore.

Later that fall Ronald Reagan was warmly received by Valley residents when he campaigned in south Texas for re-election. Conversely, the political organizers of Valley Interfaith worked hard to generate voter support for the Mondale-Ferraro Democratic presidential ticket. By then, however, their credibility was next to zero. The November election results confirmed who had won the political battle in the Rio Grande Valley. Normally, Hidalgo and Cameron counties were bastions of Democratic support. Ronald Reagan carried Cameron county (a first-ever for a Republican presidential candidate) and almost won Hidalgo county. We had turned a looming political disaster into a victory for the Reagan Administration.

I was proud of what we had achieved, but it came with a heavy personal price tag. Vehement leftist opposition to my nomination to be director of the ACTION agency in 1981 was inspired in large part by the film I was responsible for producing in 1979, critical of the Hayden-led, antinuclear movement. Now that I was engaged in another political battle with New Left activists in 1984, this victory would not come without new political scars to show for it.

As a Catholic, it was very disappointing to find my actions under attack from American bishops of my church. They didn't know me and had little true understanding of the ultimate political agenda of the Saul Alinsky-inspired radical movement they were supporting.

I have often wondered how any Catholic bishops, priests, and nuns could be so misled by a smooth operator like Ernie Cortes into believing that the IAF political network was a Christian organization. Hate and envy are among the seven deadly sins, according to those who accept the Christian faith. Yet, encouraging class warfare, seeking to destroy the reputations of people who stand in their way, arguing that the end justifies the use of any means necessary to achieve political power, are all part of the bible according to Saul Alinsky. These decidedly un-Christian principles are just as wrong whether perpetuated by a *patrone,* who treats his employees unjustly, or by a so-called leader of the dispossessed who will do whatever it takes to gain political power.

Although Cortes was thwarted in his grand ambition to use the Rio Grande Valley as the cornerstone of what he hoped would be the most powerful political network in Texas, six years later he was part of a coalition that elected a committed leftist, Ann Richards, governor of Texas. During Richards' tenure in office, Cortes has maintained a close working relationship with the governor's office. Today, this New Left leader is viewed as one of the most influential political figures in our state.

My break with the George Bush-Jim Baker wing of the Republican party had become irreversible as a result of events surrounding my tenure in the Valley as a White House representative. Jim Baker may not have been able to get me removed from that slot, but, as White House chief of staff, he was in a position to block me from going any higher in a second Reagan term.

Ed Meese had asked me if I would oversee the implementation of the Grace Commission report to reduce and streamline the federal government. I told Ed that I would welcome such an assignment. Others in the White House killed that idea. Then, the head of White House personnel asked me to serve as the ambassador in charge of the Caribbean Basin Initiative. I accepted, only to be informed later that Baker had blocked the appointment. It looked as if I were destined to spend another four years at ACTION if I intended to remain in the administration.

I decided to return home to Texas. It had been a rewarding four years. We had accomplished a lot, but I knew what others were just beginning to learn—conservatives were losing influence within the Reagan White House.

18

What Is to Be Done?

For conservatives, the period from 1985 through 1992 was one of steadily declining influence with the Republican administration. By comparison, our resilient foes on the left have made substantial gains, particularly with respect to the battle to dominate American culture. Their influence within academia, the media, and the foundation community, is widespread and deeply rooted. The words of Richard Whalen in a letter he wrote to President Nixon back in 1969 on this "cultural war" are just as timely today as when written:

> In the long run, ideas are the decisive force in a free society. It may take a generation or two, but ideas, effectively argued, change attitudes, capture institutions, and channel political energies in new directions. The survival of our system through the end of this century may depend on the struggle presently being waged in the mass communications media, the

publishing industry, and the academic-foundation complex—especially the last.

As Whalen notes, if the conservatives lose that battle, we ultimately will lose the country to the Left. You cannot talk seriously about American politics without dealing with the deeper question of what set of basic values should frame our culture.

I tried to make that case in a speech to an audience of conservatives in 1981 at a luncheon event in Washington, D.C.— hosted by the Intercollegiate Studies Institute during the first year of the Reagan administration. (ISI's mission is to extend conservative intellectual influence on the college campuses and within the ranks of the academic community.) As I said at the time, the Reagan administration had the potential to fashion a new conservative cultural majority to go along with the political majority Reagan had assembled as a result of his election in 1980.

That was my optimistic hope in 1981. When I left in 1985, I knew that the administration had failed to do this. We never effectively challenged the Left's dominance of the culture.

Things got worse during the Bush presidency. Not only did the conservative political coalition come unhinged (as R. Emmett Tyrrell, the feisty conservative publisher of the *American Spectator* pointed out in his book *The Conservative Crack-up*), but the leftist grip on the culture grew stronger.

What George Bush and his closest advisers didn't seem to understand is that America at the end of the twentieth century is in the midst of a cultural war, and whoever sits in the office of the presidency has the ability to influence the outcome of that conflict.

Conservative economist Thomas Sowell pointed out the failure of the Bush administration to recognize the seriousness of the situation in an April 2, 1990, column in the *Rocky Mountain News:* "The media and the intelligentsia are partisans in a cultural war. One of the few things worse than being in a war is being in a war and not knowing it. When the President of the United States doesn't know it, the prospects don't look good."

The example Sowell cited as evidence of the Bush administration's failure to understand what was at stake was the controversy in 1990 over taxpayer funding of obscene art by the National

Endowment for the Arts, a federal agency whose director was appointed by the president.

When some members of Congress demanded that the federal government quit subsidizing so-called art whose purpose in Sowell's words was "to insult the public's sense of decency," the Bush-appointed head of the endowment, John Frohnmeyer, defended the funding of these controversial works. Pictures of a crucifix immersed in urine, photos depicting homosexuality, and the placing of an American flag on a gallery floor for people to walk on were just a few examples of such government-funded "art."

As Sowell observed, this political battle over funding for the arts should be understood in the context of a deeper battle over the direction of our culture:

> These are not isolated episodes. They are skirmishes in a much larger war being waged for the hearts and minds of this society. The battle to break down the moral standards, the ideals and the morals of this country is being waged on a thousand fronts—from the elementary schools to the universities, from Hollywood to Broadway, from the television news to the art galleries and from the courts to Congress.
>
> This is not a conspiracy. There is simply a whole class of people who hate what this country stands for, who have contempt for its people, and who exploit every opportunity to undermine its institutions and ideals. Any resistance, or even non-cooperation, with what they are trying to do is likely to be denounced as "censorship."

This battle for America's culture is the most serious conflict within our society. As James Davison Hunter argues in his book *Culture Wars: The Struggle to Define America,* this war of ideas is one between the "progressivists" versus the forces of "orthodoxy." And the progressivists (or leftists) appear to be winning.

Take Georgetown University, for example, where both Bill Clinton and I attended college. In the old days, the university was unapologetically orthodox. Georgetown was guided in its search for truth by its distinctly religious character.

As I observed at my twenty-fifth college reunion in 1990, all that has changed at the new Georgetown. The place has a non-denominational feel about it similar to what one experiences in visiting Ivy League institutions such as Harvard and Yale that once had a religious affiliation but changed into purely secular institutions of higher learning over the years.

While a few professors, like George Carey and Fr. James Schall, S.J., still seek to pass on to the current generation of Georgetown students the basic political principles that our Founding Fathers bequeathed us, their traditionalist views are clearly out of fashion. Liberation theology and so-called Christian socialism are all the rage. The progressivists have taken over.

The political rift within our own generation was and remains deeper than the argument over what we should do about Vietnam. That issue was symbolic of a fundamental dispute involving the American culture itself. Those members of my generation who supported the other side in that war, in Sowell's words, hated "what this country stands for." Many of them have never changed their vision of "Ameri-k-a." Older and "wiser," the sixties radicals today are much better positioned to undermine the system they grew to hate long ago. Like termites eating away at the structure of a house, they can do an enormous amount of damage before one is even aware of their presence. With Bill and Hillary Clinton in the White House, the left has the further advantage of being able to place many of its adherents in positions of responsibility within the administration.

While the public facade is that this is a "centrist" Democratic administration, Bill and Hillary Rodham Clinton got their start in politics as part of the leftist protest movement against the Vietnam War. Bill Clinton also was significantly influenced by his exposure to "the best and brightest" of his generation—his fellow Rhodes Scholars from America who attended Oxford at the same time he did in the late sixties.

A story in the *Wall Street Journal* in early 1993 noted that there were more people appointed to key positions in the Clinton administration who had attended Oxford than had served in Vietnam: "The Rhodes Scholarship Trust has tallied 18 administration officials who attended Oxford. By contrast, there are only seven Vietnam veterans—most of them at the Department of Veterans Affairs."

An analysis of the early selections of key personnel reveals a combination of corporate liberal elitists with Ivy League ties (an Associated Press study found that one third of the administration's initial White House and subcabinet appointees were Ivy League graduates) and leftist activists.

The anti-military and anti-Vietnam bias of the Clinton crowd goes beyond the selection of nonveterans and former protesters to run the new administration. Beginning with the first family and extending throughout the White House staff, a perception developed in the early months of the Clinton presidency that those close to the president viewed the American military as an "enemy." Stories appeared about the Clinton daughter turning up her nose at riding to school with a military officer and about presidential aides insisting that military officers visiting the White House wear civilian clothes. A March 15, 1993, *U.S. News & World Report* story described the visit to the White House of an Army general who had been severely wounded in Vietnam and who later was a hero of the Persian Gulf War. The general "tried to exchange pleasantries with a woman in the West Wing. She angrily replied that she didn't speak to people in uniform."

Aren't these incidents, perhaps, indices and reflections of the deep-seated sentiments of the man who sits in the oval office? In a letter Bill Clinton wrote on December 3, 1969, to Colonel Eugene Holmes, director of the Arkansas ROTC program (at a time when Clinton's draft status was in question), the future president revealed his feelings at the time about the American military. Clinton wrote Colonel Holmes that he wanted to help Holmes "understand more clearly how so many fine people have come to find themselves...loathing the military, to which you and other good men have devoted years, lifetimes, of the best service you could give. To many of us, it is no longer clear what is service and what is disservice, or if it is clear, the conclusion is likely to be illegal."

My own attitude toward the American military (as is the case with other veterans) was shaped by my experiences in the army, particularly my stint in Vietnam. Isn't it logical to assume that

Bill Clinton's idea of the military was significantly influenced by the views of the anti-Vietnam protest movement he was so closely associated with at the time? If that be the case, then how difficult it must be for Bill Clinton to put all those old feelings aside now that he is the commander in chief of the armed forces.

The August 1993 issue of the *American Spectator* carried an article written by a Vietnam veteran, David Carrad, on President Clinton's visit to the Vietnam Veterans Memorial on Memorial Day 1993. The author is a Harvard Law School graduate. What he had to say in his article hit home.

He expressed sentiments about the rift within our generation which might have been uttered by me, many of those friends with whom I served in Vietnam, or those veterans I worked with in the Vietnam Veteran Leadership Program. He described why many veterans came to Washington to protest Clinton speaking on the grounds of the Memorial: "This was the monument to our generation's great fault line, the fault line that has grown wider over twenty-five years between those who went and those who didn't; between those who served and those who chickened out."

The article described how wide the split is between the assembled veterans and their commander in chief:

> And there was a second consensus among the veterans up on the hillside at LZ Slick Willie: none of us would have come to Washington [to protest his speech] had Clinton received a medical deferment for a bad knee or back, or joined the National Guard like Dan Quayle, or found some other legally proper, if morally dubious, way to stay at Oxford. What set us off was his in-your-face "I loathe the military" letter in 1969— back then, we *were* the military—and our unshakable perception that he lied to the Arkansas ROTC program in 1969, and lied again to the American people in the 1992 campaign about what he had said and done to dishonorably evade his duty to his country while we were fighting in Vietnam. There wasn't anyone on the hillside who believed that it was possible to "forget" you got an induction notice in that troubled year.

Corporate lawyers, London investment bankers, and Washington civil servants were among the two thousand Vietnam veterans who turned out on Memorial Day to demonstrate against Clinton. For many of these veterans, it was their first demonstration ever. When one of the television reporters told a veteran that his protest was "contrary to the spirit of the Wall...which was for healing the wounds of Vietnam," a vet named Terry stepped forward to voice his disagreement: "That's a myth," he said. "Why don't you go down and film the inscription on the wall and show it on television tonight? That's why we're here, and why Clinton shouldn't be. This Wall was built to honor everyone who served in Vietnam, which most emphatically does not include Mr. Clinton."

"I checked later, and Terry was right. The inscription read:

IN HONOR OF THE MEN AND WOMEN
OF THE ARMED FORCES OF THE
UNITED STATES WHO SERVED IN THE
VIETNAM WAR...OUR NATION HONORS
THE COURAGE, SACRIFICE AND
DEVOTION TO DUTY AND COUNTRY
OF ITS VIETNAM VETERANS

Not a word about "healing."

David Carrad has drawn a line in the sand. In so doing, he has linked up with many other Vietnam veterans who won't accept the inevitability of a leftist victory here at home. We have not forgotten those issues that permanently divided members of our sixties generation into warring factions.

For better or worse, the time for the final showdown between the conservatives and the New Left is drawing near. While leftist influence over American politics doesn't yet match its dominance of our culture, the countercultural forces of the sixties now have some powerful friends in the executive branch of our government. With the reelection of Bill Clinton in 1996 and the implementation of its political agenda through judicial, legislative, and executive actions, the Left could become the dominant political voice in twenty-first century America.

But our side of the sixties generation hasn't lost the war yet. In a way, we conservatives and Vietnam veterans are the American version of the Viet Cong guerrilla forces. We may not have the financial resources to match our leftist foes. Nor do we wield much influence within the major cultural institutions of our society. Politically, for all practical purposes, we are in exile with the Clinton crowd in control of the executive branch of government. Even in a conservative state like Texas, our governor (as I write this), Ann Richards, is a committed leftist whose views mirror the feminist agenda of the National Organization of Women (NOW).

Yet, for all our disadvantages, those of us who represent the new counterculture of the nineties, are still in there fighting. And we have won a few skirmishes in recent years in this ongoing cultural war with the Left. Let's build on those victories for the future.

One small victory occurred in 1990 when Vietnam veterans locked horns with Oliver Stone in a dispute over his film "Born on the Fourth of July." Over the years, Stone has become the worst offender in Hollywood when it comes to denying the validity of our service in Vietnam. Even after our Vietnam Veteran Leadership Program and other like-minded initiatives set the record straight about our pride in serving our country during that difficult war, Stone has sought to perpetuate the myth that American soldiers were little more than dehumanized murderers of innocent Vietnamese. Acclaimed as one of America's premiere filmmakers, Stone has little trouble in getting financial backing from major Hollywood studios for his highly politicized film projects. Thus far, he has made two movies on Vietnam, "Platoon" and "Born on the Fourth of July."

The latter film was based on a book by Vietnam Veterans Against the War (VVAW) activist Ron Kovic. Stone advertised his film as a true story, and the movie's message was that Vietnam permanently maimed, both physically and in spirit, a generation of young soldiers who fought there. I went to see the film because I wanted to write about it for my then regular weekly column for the *Dallas Times-Herald*. It was a powerful movie. There is no questioning Stone's talents as a cinematographer. And having Tom Cruise play Kovic was a stroke of genius on Stone's part.

But, in spite of its claim to be Kovic's true story about his service in Vietnam and his life in America afterwards as a paralyzed veteran, "Born on the Fourth of July" had a false ring to it. There was much I objected to in the film especially Stone's political message of how the Vietnam War had ruined those young Americans who served there. But it was deeper than that. One of the most powerful scenes in the movie is when Kovic visits the family of a deceased comrade in Georgia. According to the film, Kovic had accidentally killed his fellow American soldier in a fire fight with the Communists. All these years, the family believed their son had died in combat. Kovic sits in the living room of his deceased friend's family and proceeds to tell them that he—not the enemy—was responsible for the death of their son. It is a very emotional scene as you watch the reaction of the parents and the wife of the dead soldier to this news. To make the scene even more heartrending, the wife is holding a small boy, the son of the deceased soldier, who was born after his father's death in Vietnam.

I couldn't imagine an American soldier doing something like that to the family of a deceased comrade in arms. To me it seemed like a totally selfish act on Kovic's part to disrupt the lives of these people to expiate some guilt that he felt over what he had done. This would only make it harder for the young man's parents and wife to accept his loss. As it turned out, I need not have concerned myself with Kovic's actions. While the scene made for good drama, the events in question never happened. There was no such meeting between Kovic and the Georgia family of the deceased soldier, and apparently no accidental shooting by Kovic.

This was not the only fiction in Stone's self-proclaimed "true story" of a Vietnam veteran. Stone took liberties with the truth in the rendition of a number of other significant incidents in Kovic's life. Yet the American public might never have learned any of this had it not been for a group of Vietnam veterans who had seen the film. Spurred on by their anger over the message of "Born on the Fourth of July," they started digging into these alleged incidents and discovered that many of them had not happened as portrayed in the film. Certain members of the media got hold of the story, did their own investigative work, and came to the same conclusions. Stories appeared in the press that the Georgia incident had been made up and that other alleged events in the film were also suspect. This adverse publicity surfaced right before the Oscar balloting. "Born on the Fourth of July" did not win its anticipated honors at that annual event, and the credibility of Stone's film was never the same thereafter. The Vietnam veteran guerrillas had struck again.

Unfortunately, while our side of the Vietnam generation has been able to expose the falsehoods and misrepresentations of leftists like Stone, we haven't had the influence in Hollywood to see to the production of movies about the war and its aftermath which tell the other side of the story. For example, two highly acclaimed books on the war by Vietnam veterans *(Fields of Fire* and *For Self and Country)* have yet to be made into films. From the Left's viewpoint, these two books are "politically incorrect" in their portrayal of the warrior and the war. Perhaps that explains why Hollywood has shown so little interest in these particular movie projects.

Fields of Fire vividly depicts the experiences of young American soldiers thrust into combat in a war they cannot comprehend. Written by Jim Webb, it is the story of young Marines "caught in the hell of the Nam." The book opens with a description of the young men who fought in Vietnam:

> And who are the young men we are asking to go into action against such solid odds? You've met them. You know. They are the best we have. But they are not McNamara's sons, or Bundy's. I doubt they're yours. And they know they're at the end of the pipeline. That no one cares. They know.
>
> —an anonymous general
> to correspondent Arthur Hadley

Fields of Fire tells the story of a marine combat platoon based in the An Hoa basin in I Corps—young men who are just trying to survive until it is time to go home. As the *Washington Post* said about this modern classic of men at war, it "both entertains and stuns." It was the first book about the war I read after I returned. I agree with the opinion of many of my fellow veterans that *Fields of Fire* is the best novel to come out of the war. The author is a graduate of the Naval Academy who served as a marine combat commander in Vietnam. After getting his law degree from Georgetown, Webb worked on Capitol Hill and later served as secretary of the navy in the Reagan administration.

Rick Eilert, also a Marine, has written a personal story about the effects of the war and its aftermath on young soldiers who suffered crippling injuries. Entitled *For Self and Country,* Rick's book is the flip side of the Kovic story.

Eilert, who had had more than forty operations to repair the damage done to his legs by a Viet Cong mine, could easily have been consumed with hate after Vietnam like Ron Kovic. But that is not the way he reacted to his injuries. Instead, the Rick Eilert story is about a group of returning veterans who exude quiet courage in the face of serious wounds—a moving testament to the power of the human spirit to survive and overcome immense hardships. Although the book sold well and has a real human interest appeal, all efforts up to now to get a Hollywood studio to make *For Self and Country* have come to naught.

When these two fine books are made into movies, we will finally be making headway in changing the culture. Until then, the best we can hope for out of Hollywood is a diminishing number of films and television shows that depict Vietnam veterans in a negative light.

Another skirmish occurred in my home state of Texas, when we showed in May 1993 that we could put the old coalition of social and economic conservatives back together to fight a major political battle.

Our left-wing governor, Ann Richards, was seeking voter approval for a proposed amendment to the Texas constitution known as the "Robin Hood" school finance plan. This scheme to fund public education in Texas would have raised property taxes by more than $1 billion a year while redistributing an additional $400 million in local taxes from the so-called wealthier districts to the poorer school districts. This redistributionist feature of Governor Richards' proposal led it to be dubbed the Robin Hood plan for funding education.

The governor was running around the state in a "the sky is falling" posture to sell her plan: "If you don't vote yes, the schools will close." Governor Richards and Lieutenant Governor Bob

Bullock met in private with chief executive officers of major corporations doing business in Texas. Richards and Bullock made it clear to these businessmen that they were expected to make substantial contributions to pass the Robin Hood amendment if they wanted legislation of concern to their companies and/or industries to get a "fair" hearing at the state capitol. Large corporations and associations responded to these veiled threats of "political blackmail" by contributing some $2 million to pass Proposition One, the school finance amendment.

Early polls showed Robin Hood passing by a 51 to 27 percent margin. That didn't stop some of us in Texas from taking on the governor and trying to defeat this huge tax hike. My good friend Van Henry Archer from San Antonio and I organized a statewide campaign to defeat the amendment.

Easterners have traditionally viewed Texas as a state where the Wild West begins. Visions of cowboys, wildcatters, and those proverbial "long, tall Texans" are part of this mythology. Van Archer fits that last category to a tee. Van is a lanky six feet four inches, and has the courage to take on controversial, political battles most of his fellow Republican businessmen would prefer to duck.

Van Henry Archer served for seven years on the San Antonio city council, where he built a reputation as an outspoken maverick, unafraid of opposing the business establishment as well as local liberals on major issues whenever he thought they were wrong. A leader of the Reagan forces in south Texas during the 1976 and 1980 presidential primaries, he has served as the president of the San Antonio Homeowners and Taxpayers Association. Not only is Van a good friend, he is a good man to have on your side in a tough political fight. Unlike so many of the "corporate liberal" crowd who are primarily concerned with being on the winning side, Van Henry Archer is a man of principle. He is willing to fight for what he believes in.

Van and I got in touch with our fellow conservatives from throughout Texas who were as upset as we were about the Richards plan. In early March two dozen of us met at Love Field in Dallas to plan our strategy. It was like old home week for many of us who had been veterans of the Reagan Revolution and who hadn't worked together since. Those assembled were in complete agreement that this measure had to be defeated to reverse the leftist drift of our state government.

Calling ourselves Texans Against Robin Hood Taxes, we organized a statewide, volunteer-led committee to defeat Proposition One. We kept our message simple: The Robin Hood amendment will raise your taxes while doing nothing to improve the quality and accountability of education.

While spending on public education in Texas has more than doubled over the past decade, achievement scores have fallen substantially. Texas now ranks forty-sixth among the states in average SAT scores. Texans were being asked to go along with yet another hike in property taxes at a time when our state already had the dubious reputation of being a high property tax state. Moreover, there were no signs that we would see any improvement in the quality of education with this added expenditure of tax dollars.

Van and I were convinced that we could defeat the Robin Hood amendment if we could get our message to the public.

It wasn't easy.

While the proponents spent two million dollars on an expensive media campaign to sell the amendment, Texans Against Robin Hood Taxes struggled to raise a meager thirty thousand to fight Proposition One.

The pro-Robin Hood forces had a bevy of high-priced political consultants running their campaign. Meanwhile, we were mostly volunteers, taking time off from our regular jobs to fight the amendment. We countered the slick television and radio ads selling Robin Hood, with hand-out sheets and a four-page tabloid produced by John Mauldin, a businessman and communications specialist from Arlington, Texas. Charley Johnson, a conservative from the Panhandle region who had migrated to Dallas County for business reasons, volunteered to write most of the copy for the tabloid. Some 250,000 tabloids were printed and distributed by grassroots organizations, ranging from taxpayers associations to the Christian Coalition.

Whitey Lingerfelt, a retired chief master sergeant from the air force, saw to it that our literature got out to volunteers scattered throughout the state. Barbara Adamson, a Reagan conservative from Dallas, did a magnificent job scheduling Van Archer and me as we traveled across Texas carrying our message. Bruce Woody, a retired military officer and lawyer, along with his wife Jan, became full-time volunteers in our campaign to defeat the proposed constitutional amendment. Hundreds of others joined as volunteers in this fight against higher taxes.

For the first time since the Reagan era, a coalition of economic conservatives and social conservatives in Texas was working together on a major campaign.

As Van Archer and I traveled the state (appearing on radio talk shows, meeting with local media, and working with grassroots leaders), we began to notice a rippling effect from our efforts. We could sense that people were fed up with high taxes and an educational bureaucracy more interested in self-preservation than in reversing the decline in the quality of public education in Texas. Grassroots opposition to Robin Hood appeared seemingly out of nowhere. Individuals and small businessmen ran ads in their local newspapers against the proposition. A "fax" campaign was initiated by John Mauldin and his brother Ron. One group in Laredo even ran a clever, low budget television ad against the amendment, with one of its members dressed up as Robin Hood.

The people were tired of being lied to by the politicians in Austin. Two years earlier, Governor Richards had relied on a slick and expensive media campaign to sell Texans on a state lottery. At the time the voters were led to believe that the resulting revenues would go to "help the kids" by being spent on education. Instead, our elected officials used the lottery revenues to give pay raises to state employees. When we pointed this out in the campaign, voters were furious. They were not about to be fooled again. All over Texas people began to demand that their representatives in Austin use the lottery monies to help equalize education funding.

We hammered on the theme that higher taxes weren't the answer and offered a sensible alternative which provided for real educational reform without raising property taxes.

On May 1, Texas voters rejected the Robin Hood amendment by 63 to 37 percent in a stunning defeat for the governor and the state education establishment. The tax revolt gained new momentum in this David over Goliath victory for the middle class. As I said after the election, that victory demonstrated once again that we are not yet a nation of sheep.

Another skirmish in the ongoing cultural war occurred when Pat Buchanan led the fight to force John Frohnmeyer out as director of the National Endowment for the Arts. In that position, Frohnmeyer had defended governmental funding of sacrilegious and obscene art. Mounting a conservative challenge to George Bush in the 1992 Republican presidential primaries, Buchanan attacked the administration for its use of taxpayers' dollars for art that was an affront to our basic values. Shortly thereafter, Frohnmeyer was forced to resign. Buchanan's campaign as an outsider had succeeded on at least this one front.

When it comes to the media, conservatives aren't completely shut out. Talk radio has been a boon to the conservative movement in getting our message directly to the American public without first forcing it through the liberal-dominated mainstream media filtration process. I have had daily radio programs on stations in Waco, Texas, in 1985-86, and in Dallas in 1991, and I saw firsthand the difference it made in getting coverage of important issues that would otherwise go unreported or reported only from a liberal perspective.

Talk shows are a natural for conservatives in an era in which the dominant culture is leftist. Look at the huge impact that Rush Limbaugh has had with his nationally syndicated, radio and television shows. Now, the conservative radio and television host has followed up that success with best-selling books on the conservative philosophy. He drives the leftists crazy, plus he has been a great supporter of Vietnam veterans. Rush Limbaugh is a conservative guerrilla warrior of the airwaves.

Conservative publications such as *National Review, American Spectator, Human Events,* and *Chronicles of Culture* are indispensable to our movement in providing intellectual ammunition in this ongoing cultural and political war. Magazines with a broader appeal such as *Reader's Digest, Forbes,* and the editorial pages of the *Wall Street Journal* reach millions of readers on a regular basis with incisive analysis from a conservative perspective. Tom Bethell, Pat Buchanan, Sam Francis, John Fund, Paul Gigot, Irving Kristol, Bob Novak, Paul Craig Roberts, Joe Sobran, R. Emmett Tyrrell and George Will are well-respected and widely-read conservative columnists who have assumed the role that William F. Buckley, seemed to occupy all by himself back in the early days of the conservative movement.

Conservatives also are busily at work trying to correct the leftist imbalance in the world of foundations. The Capitol Research Center, founded by Willa Johnson and now run by Terry Scanlon, does an extremely effective job in exposing the liberal dominance of most of the major foundations. Their good work has resulted in individuals and corporations paying closer attention to their charitable contribution programs to make sure that pro-free enterprise money isn't being used to fund socialist causes. Mike Joyce at the Bradley Foundation has been a leader in the effort to encourage the redirection of foundation spending away to more worthwhile causes.

The Heritage Foundation, the premiere conservative policy institute, provides excellent research on domestic and foreign policy issues which it makes available to key opinion leaders on a timely basis. Led by longtime conservative leaders Ed Feulner and Phil Truluck, Heritage has replaced the more liberal Brookings Institute as the most influential public policy organization in Washington.

The American Conservative Union, founded in 1964 and headed for the last decade by the superb political strategist David Keene, has grown from fewer than 20,000 members to more than 500,000 in recent years. With its large membership and capable staff, ACU serves ably as the conservative movement's Washington lobby. It's annual Conservative Political Action Conference, co-sponsored by more than sixty organizations each February, is viewed annually by millions of Americans on C-SPAN. The ACU has been particularly effective working on Capitol Hill—briefing congressmen, organizing coalitions, and on occasion focusing enormous public pressure on Congress through millions of letters and phone calls.

The Rockford Institute, based in the heartland of America (Rockford, Illinois), is gaining renown for its important work on cultural and family issues. This conservative policy institute has led the way in warning our citizenry of the dangers posed by the breakdown of family life and the growing rootlessness of American society. Led by Allan Carlson, Rockford also is publisher of the *Chronicles of Culture,* edited by Tom Fleming.

One of the original leaders of the conservative movement, Stan Evans, runs a Washington institute to train young, conservative journalists. The former editor of the *Indianapolis News,* Stan has graduated thousands of young journalists from his school, many of whom have gone on to success.

Intercollegiate Studies Institute (ISI) concentrates on providing conservative academic offerings—political theory, economics, history, and philosophy—to students on college campuses across America. It now has more than 50,000 members who receive campus publications. This is particularly valuable to students who find themselves at odds with their politically correct professors. Unfortunately, for the students of the nineties, many of their college teachers are unrepentant radicals from the sixties who are just as closeminded today as they were back then—when they wouldn't tolerate any dissent from their position on Vietnam. Ken Cribb, who got his start in the sixties as a campus representative for ISI, now heads up that organization and has done a terrific job of building an effective network of campus conservatives.

What all this suggests is that we have enough conservative firepower on our side these days to mount an effective counterattack against the New Left. Even though we are missing the kind of political leadership Barry Goldwater and Ronald Reagan provided in previous decades, we conservatives can still win important political victories if we unite social and economic conservatives under a common banner. Columnist Paul Gigot of the *Wall Street Journal* succinctly described the need to reconcile genuine differences within the Republican party in order to build a permanent, political majority. In his December 18, 1992, column, Gigot wrote: "Social conservatives aren't always going to agree with younger libertarians. But the task of political leadership (as Ronald Reagan and Bill Clinton know) is to forge a coalition in which many views can coexist."

Unfortunately, in the post-Reagan period, conservatives all too often have become like "a house divided." If we continue to fight among ourselves, we run the risk of losing sight of the major threat—the potential leftist takeover of our culture and political system. Libertarians, traditionalists, and neoconservatives have worked together effectively in the past, particularly when it came to electing Ronald Reagan and in opposing the fatal flaws of the liberal culture. So, why can't we band together once more behind a common set of shared beliefs?

And, if we are to succeed, we will need to rally the Vietnam veterans one more time. Just because a Vietnam war protester happens to be the first member of our generation to occupy the White House, doesn't mean the New Left has won the war. Clinton doesn't measure up to the high standards demanded of a president in these difficult times. The American people already sense this. When they get fed up with Clinton (as they surely will), they will look elsewhere for leadership. The unanswered question is whether our side of the Vietnam generation will step forward to answer that call.

The veterans are with us in spirit. Whether they join us in this particular fight depends on us. Ronald Reagan made Vietnam veterans feel right at home. In a way, he helped bring them home. With them as part of our coalition, we can forge a new majority and reclaim our country from the Left.

Afterword

On June 18, 1994, the Republican Party of Texas elected Tom Pauken its chairman. This was not without extraordinary labor on the new chairman's part and outcries of pain by exemplars of the old way of doing things—or not doing them.

Suffice it to say that no one viewing these proceedings, whomever he backed for chairman, expected that the Republican Party would remain as before. No one at all acquainted with Tom Pauken's career—certainly no reader of this candid book—could expect any such thing. It would be contrary to nature.

The nature of Tom Pauken, if one who has known him for two decades may venture an unsolicited opinion, is to look at a thing that needs doing, and then to go out and do it: meticulously, confidently, and often enough with sparkling success.

The Texas GOP, since it became prominent in the 1960s and began to drain off disaffected Democratic conservatives, has benefited from the ministrations of many hands. It may be that none of these hands has displayed a surer grasp of political principle—or greater stubbornness in holding tight to it—than Tom Pauken's. The new state party chairman represents, as Ronald Reagan at the national level represented, the politics of change. Conservative change.

The British have a political term—"wet"—that is useful for characterizing politicians soft on principles, innately disposed to give way and give way until hardly anything is left of what they initially said they were promoting or defending. True, no democratic politician, such is the variety of interests he must compose, ever gets his way 100 percent; prudent and timely compromise is at the heart of all politics. But wetness as a way of political life means the destruction of politics itself. It means there is almost nothing that the sopping wet won't toss overboard, concede, throw away while somebody is shouting at them, calling them names, berating them for insensitivity.

There is no coherent policy left after all this; no one is happy, and things end up worse than ever. Ronald Reagan's words beat on our ears with greater and greater force: "If not us, who? If not now, when?".

The central myth of Texas history is the Alamo. A myth in its classic sense is not some blithe tale about gamboling gods and goddesses. Rather, a myth is the recounting of an incident, or a series of incidents—whether legendary or purely historical is beside the point—that the tellers have appropriated to themselves, because, in the telling, who they are becomes clearer and clearer.

The myth of the Alamo—a concrete historical occurrence with flesh-and-blood characters—centers on the resolution of the men who sold their lives in order to make Texas. There were no wets at the Alamo: no compromisers, no doers of deals. There were only soldiers, and soldiers' wives and dependents, who shared a vision and a sacrificial spirit. The vision was that Texas should be free; the chosen sacrificial victims were—themselves. Nothing mattered more—not life, not property, not the prospect of feet up in a tavern and a comfortable pipe—than the free Texas that was in their hearts and minds.

Texans have never let go of this resplendently factual myth; not yet they haven't. It speaks to them at the darkest times, when all seems lost and nervous hands fumble about for the flag of truce. Texans remember that at such a moment Col. William Barret Travis, in response to a peremptory demand for surrender, fired a cannon shot in the general direction of Santa Anna's army.

The plight of Texas, despite cultural and political crisis, is hardly so desperate today. Still, the example—a cannon belching smoke and flame, a projectile hurtling through the air—commands, so I would judge, amazing sympathy. Simply to stand, refusing every temptation to give way, every emolument offered— is not this something?

Tom Pauken, though I have not asked him expressly, clearly thinks it is something, because standing has become his specialty; standing and speaking what is in his heart and on his mind. The Texas Republican Party, under his chairmanship, has interesting times in store for it; and not just the party either, I would surmise.

—WILLIAM MURCHISON
The Dallas Morning News

Index

SHELBYVILLE-SHELBY COUNTY
PUBLIC LIBRARY